Praise for *Buck*

"Frequently brilliant and always engaging . . . It takes great skill to render the wide variety of characters, male and female, young and old, that populate a memoir like *Buck*. [Asante is] at his best when he sets out into the city of Philadelphia itself. In fact, that city is the true star of this book. Philly's skateboarders, its street-corner philosophers and its tattoo artists are all brought vividly to life here. . . . Asante's memoir will find an eager readership, especially among young people searching in books for the kind of understanding and meaning that eludes them in their real-life relationships. . . . A powerful and captivating book."

—*Los Angeles Times*

"The book's strength lies in Asante's vibrant, specific observations, and, at times, the percussive prose that captures them. The author's fluid, filmic images of black urban life feel unique and disturbing."

—*Kirkus Reviews*

"Asante's noir chronicle is imaginative, powerful, and electric, written with passion and conviction."

—*Publishers Weekly*

"This is an inspiring story about perseverance and finding purpose that is sure to appeal to readers interested in hip-hop, black studies, and American culture in general."

—*Booklist*

"A story of surviving and thriving with passion, compassion, wit, and style. MK Asante's work is very necessary to us all."

—MAYA ANGELOU

"MK Asante's *Buck* takes the daily words of the American streets and forges something low and lovely. Angry, profane and beautiful, it honors the best of hip-hop's literary canon by producing a work worthy of inclusion. Here is crack-era Philadelphia flipped into a phrase which we've so long needed, but so rarely heard."

—TA-NEHISI COATES, author of *The Beautiful Struggle*

"MK Asante takes back the 90s black American experience that we've seen chopped, screwed, and co-opted and gives it an original voice singing a song that will force all of America to face what it has become and remember what it could be."

—EDDIE HUANG, author of *Fresh Off the Boat*

"Written with poignant and at times pugnacious prose, Asante details how things fell apart for him as he tried to negotiate the ghetto, growing up fatherless with a mother in a mental institution. How he emerges intact and in control is well worth the read."

—*Philadelphia Weekly*

BUCK

BUCK

A Memoir

M K Asante

SPIEGEL & GRAU TRADE PAPERBACKS
NEW YORK

Buck is a work of nonfiction. Some names and identifying details have been changed.

2014 Spiegel & Grau Trade Paperback Edition

Published in the United States by Spiegel & Grau, an imprint of Random House, a division of Random House LLC, a Penguin Random House Company, New York.

Spiegel & Grau and the House colophon are registered trademarks of Random House LLC.

Originally published in hardcover in the United States by Spiegel & Grau, an imprint of Random House, a division of Random House LLC, in 2013.

LIBRARY OF CONGRESS CATALOGING-IN-PUBLICATION DATA
Asante, Molefi K.
Buck : a memoir / MK Asante.
pages cm.
ISBN 978-0-8129-8362-3 (alk. paper) — ISBN 978-0-679-64545-0 (eBook)
Asante, Molefi K., 1981. 2. African American authors—Biography.
3. Philadelphia (Pa.)—Biography. I. Title.
PS3601.S26Z46 2013
811'.6—dc23 2012042211
[B]

Title-page photograph: © iStockphoto.com

Printed in the United States of America on acid-free paper

www.spiegelandgrau.com

19 18 17 16 15 14 13

Book design by Dana Leigh Blanchette

To all the young bucks.

"Be patient and tough; someday this pain will be useful to you."

—OVID

BUCK

1

The Fall

The fall in Killadelphia. Outside is the color of corn bread and blood. Change hangs in the air like the sneaks on the live wires behind my crib. Me and my big brother, Uzi, in the kitchen. He's rolling a blunt on top of the *Source,* the one with Tyson on the cover rocking a kufi, ice-grilling through the gloss. Uzi can roll a blunt with his eyes closed.

Cracks, splits, busts.

"The rawest crews in Philly are all three letters," he tells me. I read the cover through the tobacco guts and weed flakes: "The Rebirth of Mike Tyson: 'I'm Not Good. I'm Not Bad. I'm Just Trying to Survive in this World.'"

Awaking crews in a rude fashion
On they ass like Mike Tyson at a beauty pageant*

* "Wreck Your Ears (Can Do)," The B.U.M.S. (Brothas Under Madness), 1995.

I do this—spit lyrics to songs under my breath—all day, every day. The bars just jump out of me no matter where I am or what I'm doing. It's like hip-hop Tourette's.

Dumps, spreads, evens.

"JBM—Junior Black Mafia. Of course us, UPK—Uptown Killaz. PHD—Play Hero and Die."

Tears, licks, wraps.

"HRM—Hit Run Mob. EAM—Erie Ave. Mobsters. ABC—Another Bad Creation."

Folds, rolls, tucks. Another perfect blunt, jawn looks like a paintbrush.

Jawn can mean anything—person, place, or thing. Sometimes if we're telling a story and don't want people to know what we're talking about, we'll plug *jawn* in for everything. *The other day I was at the jawn around the corner with the young jawn from down the street. We get to the jawn, right, and the ngh at the door is all on his jawn, not knowing I had that jawn on me. Man, it was about to be on in that jawn.*

"Then you got all the songs: AFD—'Ass for Days,' CIA—'Crack in America,' FAG—'Fake Ass Gangsta,' HAA—'Here's Another Asshole,' OPP—'Other People's Property,' PWA—'Pussy Weed Alcohol,' and Philly's own PSK—'Park Side Killas.' "

"Schoolly D . . ." I hear Schoolly D's voice in my head. "PSK, we makin that green . . . ," I start.

"People always say, 'What the hell does that mean?' " Uzi finishes.

"P is for the people who can't understand how one homeboy became a man . . ." Both bopping to the subs in our domes. *Boom, bap bap, boom-bap.*

"S is for the way we scream and shout . . ."

"One by one . . ." He lands a soft hook on my cheek.

"I knock 'em out!" we both rap, laughing as he follows his punch through. I try to tap his chin but can't reach.

"Your arms too short to box with God," he says like Big Daddy Kane in "Mortal Combat," Uzi's anthem.

Uzi is the color of walnuts and has a long, sharp face like the African masks my dad hangs up everywhere. His name is Daahoud, my parents call him Daudi, and the hood calls him Uzi. He's got a bunch of other names too, like some superhero: Oohwop, Daa-Ooh, Uzito, Wop da Culture, Cool D, Pinch P, Big Ooh, Barkalark, Droptimus Rhyme, Big Fly, and Stilt the Kilt.

A fast knock hits the window.

"Who dat?" Uzi says, running the flame across the blunt, drying it. I push the window open, cool air rushes in.

"Yo, what up, Malo?"

"It's Ted!" I yell back to Uzi. "What up, Ted?" Ted is Uzi's best friend. He's like yay high, albino light, and bulldog stocky. He's got a pug nose with freckles spread across it like crumbs. His nicknames are Ted Money, Reds the Ghost, Teddy Rux, and Thiefadore Burgalor.

"Where ya brother at?" Gold ropes dangle over his Tommy Hill hoodie, and the Beijing dye on his shape-up makes his hairline look airbrushed.

"Right here," I say, leaning out the window. Uzi puts the blunt behind his ear. Pushes me aside.

"Ted Money, waddup?"

Ted checks both coasts like a lookout boy. "We got a car," he says, hitchhiker thumb shooting backward. "A Johnny!"

"Who's we?"

"Me, D-Rock, and you . . . if you down to roll?"

"Hell yeah," Uzi says, no hesitation, then pivots toward the door. I follow him like his shadow.

And this is how it always goes: me following Uzi in everything, everywhere, like his little black Jansport, covered in Marks-A-Lot, strapped tight to his back—koala style. Anywhere, anyplace. He does it, I do it. He tries it, fuck it, I'm trying it. He can, shit, why can't I? Sometimes I even duck like him under doorways, even though he's way taller and I don't need to duck. I guess I just do it because Uzi's more than my big brother, he's my idol. I don't care that he's taller, and older, and smarter. I wouldn't even really know his age if old people weren't always bringing that shit up, talking 'bout "you can't do this, you can't do that"—why?

"Because he's sixteen and you're twelve," they say.

I follow him to sweaty Badlands house parties that always end in crazy, shirtless rumbles with everybody howling "Norf-side! Norf-side!" in the middle of the street. To Broad and Rockland to cop dime bags from one of the dusty bodegas with nothing but baking soda and expired Bisquick on the shelves. To freestyle cyphers on South Street that the nut-ass police always break up for no reason. To crack on jawns getting off the El at 69th Street, like, "Yo, shawty, let me holla at you for a minute." To scale the fence to watch Sad Eye, the Jordan of street ball, hoop at 16th and Susquehanna. To skate the ledges and steps at Love Park until we get chased away by the cops. To bomb the Orange Line subway with Sharpies and Kiwi polish sticks.

And now, to joyride through Philly in a stolen wheel.

Being with Uzi makes me feel invincible, like nothing bad can happen to us, like nothing and nobody can hurt us. I feel unfuckwitable.

I can see us now, peeling off, sound system booming louder than bombs, rolling down 5th Street, turning heads as we catch the breeze. This is how freedom must taste.

"Chill," Uzi tells me, pushing me back. "Not this time." Turns his shoulder.

"I'm down, though," I say, inching forward.

"I know," he says. Grabs both my arms. "But not this time." He lets go. Palms the doorknob.

Now I'm picturing the car spin, all of us laughing, half hanging out the window, tires screaming as we bust victory donuts.

"I'm coming!" I shout loud enough for Ted to hear.

"Ma-lo!" Uzi shoves me into the radiator. His eyes tell me to chill. "I'll be back." Shuts the door.

Through the window, I watch them sprint toward a blue Chevy Celebrity. Jailbreak joyful, their stride says they'll never come back.

Ten minutes later—

Uzi and Ted explode back into the crib looking like they just saw a ghost. I'm still in the kitchen, still mad about not rolling.

"Oh shit, oh shit, oh shit!" they gasp, jetting right by me.

"Get in your room, Malo!" Uzi yells. They bolt upstairs,

doors slamming everywhere like a haunted house. Before I hit the stairs, I peek out the window—*oh shit, oh shit, oh shit!* There's a light show in front of the crib. Reds, blues, and a gang of whites. The most cops I've ever seen.

I hit the stairs, three at a time. I'm almost at the top when an earthquake hits the house. I spin around to see the front door fly off like back draft. It lifts, then slams hard against the wood floor. Black boots trample it like a bridge. The whole house is heaving. The sound of everything crashing, breaking. A battering ram leads a tsunami of blue in. They flood the house. Clenched Glocks pointing every which way.

"Police! Get down! Down!" a flushed red face yells. My fingers freeze on the banister as the tide climbs the stairs.

"Down! Down!" I'm stuck. Can't move. Guns glaring at me, steely-eyed. Pee shoots down my leg.

"Fuck-ing down!" Dripping. They pry me from the banister. Drag me down the steps like a rag doll. Clothes ripping. My head hits every step like a mallet over a xylophone. When I get to the bottom, everything sounds gargled like I'm underwater, drowning.

Officer Red Face is six inches from my grill. "Where is he?" he screams through tight lips. Grabs me. "Where is he?" Shakes me. "Where?" Shaking the fuck out of me. Everything's getting pixelated.

Red Face lets go, charges up the steps.

My eyes clear, refocus. I make out Uzi kneeling at the top of the steps, elbows over face, nightsticks marching on his head, hands, ribs, neck, back, everywhere. I feel every blow like they're beating me too. I sprint up the stairs again, but they swallow me, holding me down, twisting my arms like a pretzel.

I hear my favorite voice—"Get the fuck off my little brother"—before I black out.

2

By the Time I Get to Arizona

Uzi tells me they tried to throw the book at him.

"You're lucky you're still a minor," my pops tells him. "If you were eighteen, you'd be in the penitentiary." He fills the doorway to Uzi's room like a prison guard. I'm sitting on the bed, long-faced, watching Uzi pack for a one-way trip to Arizona.

My dad's Afro is thick and flat at the back like how Muhammad Ali's jawn was back in the day. He's wearing a black and gold dashiki. He's got a dashiki for every day of the year.

"I'm African," he told Uzi and Ted the other day on the porch. Ted calls Pops "Dr. Africa." "That's why I wear African clothes."

"But you're from Georgia," Uzi said.

"Being born in Georgia doesn't make me an American any more than being born in an oven makes a cat a biscuit."

"Huh?"

"There's an African proverb that says, 'No matter how long a log sits in a river, it will never become a crocodile.' That means that even in a foreign habitat, a snail never loses its shell. Even in America, I'm still African."

"Here he goes." Uzi shook his head. "Always in his Afrocentric bag."

The newspapers call our father "the father of Afrocentricity" because he created it.

My third eye is my rail, on this L of thought
With Afrocentric stamps I'm mailin thoughts*

Pops is always preaching Afrocentricity. He was a Church of Christ minister way back when, one of those child preachers, and he still sounds like he's in the pulpit when he talks about black people, white people, and the struggle. I remember this debate he took me to at East Stroudsburg University a few years back: him vs. Cornel West vs. Arthur Schlesinger. It was packed, standing room only. I remember how West, this cool black dude with a big Afro and a tight three-piece suit, talked with his hands flying fast like he was conducting an orchestra. And how Schlesinger, this old white guy with hair the color of milk and a red bow tie, sounded like a statue. I remember the cheers, the boos, the ad-libs. Most of all, though, I remember how dope my pops was: his passion, energy, confidence, intelligence. Half the time I didn't even know what he was talking about—*hegemony . . . pedagogy . . . subverting the dominant paradigm*—but I was proud.

* "All Night Long," Common, 1996.

—

Back then I didn't get it, but now I think I do. Afrocentricity basically means that black people should view the world through our own black eyes. It's like the poster my dad has framed in the hallway that says, "A people without knowledge of their past is like a tree with no roots."

Hit the Earth like a comet, invasion.
Nas is like the Afrocentric Asian, half-man, half-amazin*

Our crib is mad Afrocentric: naked African statues standing everywhere, ritual masks ice-grilling down from the walls, portraits of Martin, Malcolm, Harriet. From the wallpaper to the plates, everything is stamped with Africa.

Even my favorite porn series, *My Baby Got Back,* is made by a company called Afro-Centrix Productions. "Beauties that give up the booty," the box under my bed says. Mr. Marcus, Lexington Steele, and loudmouthed Wesley Pipes nailing Nubian queens like Janet Jacme, Obsession, Midori, Monique, and Lacey Duvalle in doggy style, reverse cowgirl, and missionary.

I tell Pops about the other Afro-Centrix and he's disgusted. *Say what?* But he's the one who's always talking about how black people should have their own stores, own banks, own schools—shouldn't we have our own porn studios too? What's more Afrocentric than black pussy?

* "It Ain't Hard to Tell," Nas, 1996.

—

Uzi doesn't really get down with Afrocentricity. I think he's still mad about the whole *Star Wars* thing from when we were little. Uzi used to love *Star Wars* and he kept begging my parents for a Luke Skywalker action figure. Finally my dad took him to Toys R Us. They came back—Uzi was heated.

"He got me Lando Calrissian!" Uzi said.

"Who?"

"Exactly! Nobody knows who he is. Lando Calrissian!"

"Who that?"

"Fucking Billy Dee Williams! The corny black dude. He has no gun, no weapon, no special powers, and he talks like he's in a goddamn Colt 45 commercial, like"—he lowered his voice—" 'the power of Colt 45 . . . works every time.' "

"They didn't have Luke?"

"They had everybody—Luke, Obi-Wan, Han Solo—but Dad wouldn't get them because they're white."

So now Uzi's in his closet deciding what to take with him to Arizona.

"Make sure you leave this room better than you found it," my dad says, scoping the mess.

"Whateva," Uzi sighs, and tosses a shirt into his duffle.

"What'd you say?" My dad moves closer. I see his face clenching, like he wants to slap the shit out of Uzi. He won't, though, because Uzi's his stepson. Now if it were me, I'd be ducking haymakers. Uzi steps out of the closet. They're a swing away from each other. My brother, at 6'6", Michael Jordan's height, towers over my pops, who might be 5'7"—Spud Webb. Pops ain't no slouch, though. He's southern stocky, used to chase chickens and wrestle swamp thangs and chop firewood back in the day.

"What"—Uzi tilts his head like one side weighs more—"eva."

Pops swallows hard. They eye each other down like the cowboys in the black-and-white Westerns my uncle John loves watching—toothpicks plugged into stone faces, beat-up brims, ashy steel toes.

I love a good fight, but I don't want to see this. One day when Uzi was real mad at my dad, he told me if it ever came down to it, he'd fight my pops like "a ngh on the street." I don't want to see that, and I know deep down Uzi doesn't want that either, but he's a cannon. He's got a Rasheed Wallace temper, so hot you can fry bacon on it.

"Finish packing. Be downstairs ready to go in thirty. You're not welcome in this house anymore."

"Man, I don't give a fuck!"

"Don't you use that language with me, boy," Pops says, pointing at Uzi, eyes on fire.

"You Malo dad, not mine." Uzi moves in closer. "Don't get it twisted." I can see the veins in Uzi's neck pulse like little lightning bolts, striking on every word.

"Pack. Your. Bags," my dad blows out. He turns to me. "Downstairs!"

"Why?"

"Because I—"

"Damn, I can't chill with my lil' brother before y'all kick

me out?" Uzi jumps in. "You said I ain't coming back, right? Well, at least let me say bye to my lil' brother."

"Yea, c'mon," I add.

"Thirty minutes!" He storms out. Uzi kicks the door shut.

"Can't stand him," Uzi says, scrunching up his face. "Wish I lived with my real dad. That ngh right there, my real pops"—shakes his head into his fist in awe—"is cool as shit. Lets me do whatever the fuck I want."

Whenever Uzi gets into it with my dad, he starts talking about Bob, his dad.

"Bob is the truth," he says.

No he ain't, I think.

I've heard all this before, but I listen like it's new music. In my mind, though, this song is played out. He sings about how Bob runs shit in Harlem, from One-two-fifth to the Heights; how everybody calls him "the mayor of the ghetto"; how he's always rocking the fly shit before everyone else—fitteds, jerseys, fedoras; how he curses up a storm, all types of *fuck*s and *shit*s and *bitch*es—hurricane slang.

But the other night, while Uzi was locked up, I heard the unofficial lyrics to the song. The ones hidden in Uzi's stomach, I guess. They said that Bob is a junky, all strung out on heroin; that he beat the everything out of my mom every day they were together, like Ike Turner did Tina; and that my mom's neighbor, a priest, put a gun in Bob's mouth and told him if he ever touched my mom again he'd be "summoned to appear before his maker." My mom told me this secret music from her chair, Egyptian pillow resting on her stomach. I was kneeling next to her, holding her soft hands, soaking up these blues.

"He would beat me and beat me until my eyes were purple and swollen shut." She cried as she told me. I hugged her with all I had: arms, heart, body, and soul. I want to protect her from everything, from all the evil in this cold world. I think about the man who beat her and bite my bottom lip so hard it bleeds. I think about using my dad's double-barreled shotgun on Bob—about taking it from his closet, loading it with buckshots just like Pops taught me last summer after our crib got robbed, and squeezing. Uzi doesn't know that I know this.

"Bob is *that* ngh," Uzi says.

Fuck Bob! is what I really want to say, but this is Uzi's last day in Philly and I don't want him to bounce on a bad note—so I press mute.

My parents are in the kitchen waiting to take Uzi to the airport. They're mad because Uzi keeps getting in trouble. They get him out, but he gets right back in. They keep saying he's playing with fire.

He gets expelled from all the schools: Ivy Leaf for telling some girl "Suck my dick, bitch" in the middle of math class; Piney Woods, this black military school in Mississippi, for breaking some kid's nose; and a bunch of other places. He even gets booted from the last-chance schools—the ones with names like Second Chance and Fresh Start—so now my parents don't know what the fuck to do.

The day after Uzi got locked up they called a family meeting. They sat us down and talked about the struggle, about the sacrifices our ancestors made, and about how they came up. They asked us all these questions about their upbringing, then answered before we could respond.

Do you know where we came from?

DAD: A one-room shack in Valdosta, Georgia. I was the oldest boy of sixteen children. Sixteen of us in a shack the size of a pigeon coop, on the banks of the Okefenokee Swamp and Withlacoochee River.

MOM: The projects in Bed-Stuy, Brooklyn. I was the oldest girl of three. We all slept in the same bed. Single mom.

Do you know what it was like back then for us?

DAD: I started working on the plantation when I was six. Picking cotton for white folks. I picked more than I weighed, working under the hot Georgia sun from can't see in the morning to can't see at night. The thorns around the bolls would leave my hands cracked and bloody. We were sharecroppers who never got a share. Separate restaurants, separate water fountains, separate toilets, separate schools, churches, neighborhoods. The only thing that blacks and whites shared in Valdosta were mosquitoes.

MOM: I started working when I was eight: scrubbing floors and toilets for white families in Long Island. It showed me just how poor we were. Dirt.

Do you know how hard it was?

DAD: I was eleven when I got my first job as a shoeshine boy at a white barbershop. I just took my wooden shoe box and went inside the shop and asked the owner if I could set up and shine shoes. He said, "Yeah, boy, just give me fifteen cents on every quarter you make." Shining white people's shoes was a guaranteed position; after all, it was nonthreatening and subservient. So I was not surprised that I got the job; other than working in the fields, it was probably the only job that I could have gotten at the time. My first customer, a young white man in his twenties with black shoes, sat in the chair near the window, and I took out my polish, my rag, and toothbrush. When I finished, instead of paying me, he spat in my face.

MOM: I saw my mother raped. We lived on the third floor of a rooming house on Vanderbilt Avenue. "Yell for help, yell for help," my mother told me as the man broke down the door to our room. I ran to the window and looked down on the dark street where nothing seemed like it was moving. I opened my mouth wide but nothing came out. No voice, no cry, no nothing.

The refrain: *If we made it from all that—from projects and plantations—what's your problem?* It's not just Uzi either. My cousin Kadir from the Bronx got knocked a week after Uzi did for robbing the subway platform.

"The subway platform?" I asked my aunt on the phone.

"Yes, he robbed everyone who was waiting for the A train at ten-thirty in the morning. I'm convinced he's lost his goddamn mind."

They're sending Uzi to Arizona to live with my uncle Jabbar. Bar's cool. He's a former Golden Gloves champ who sparred with Muhammad Ali back in the day. He always rocks a gold chain, pinky nugget ring, and a hustla's grin. Cadillac slick, he looks just like Tubbs from *Miami Vice*.

Last time I saw him, on Thanksgiving, he pulled me to the side.

"You getting any ass yet?" he asked, submarine voice. I just laughed. His thick hands pulled me close.

"Huh?" He studied me, tightening his grip. I nodded a lil' nod. "My boy!" He scrubbed the top of my head like a lotto scratch-off. "Life is all about ass . . . You're either covering it, laughing it off, kicking it, kissing it, busting it for some white man at the job, or getting some!" I cracked up.

"Just remember," he said. "Sex is like riding a bike: you gotta keep pumping if you want to go anywhere . . . Lemme ask you something else?"

"What's up, Unc?"

"You eating pussy yet?" He grabbed me.

"Come on, Unc," squiggling out of his grip.

"Let me smell your breath." He chased as I jetted out of the room.

He found me in my room.

"Put your shit up," he said, putting his hands, like boulders, in front of his grill. He threw a jab at me. "Fuck you gon' do, nephew?" Sizing me up like a fitted hat. I jumped out of my seat.

"Gotta be ready for anything." Touched my chin with another jab. "C'mon now, put your shit up." I threw my hands up. He caught me again—bang. "Keep 'em up, young buck. Up! Protect them pussy-eating lips."

I moved them up. His fist on my ribs. My hands fell like they were asleep. His fist on my chin. He picked me apart, then showed me how to hold my hands.

"Stand strong, feet shoulder width apart, like this." Planted his feet, fixed my stance. "And if you ever want to kiss a ngh good night," staring into his right fist, "swing it like this. Land it right there," landing it slo-mo on my face.

I pulled back and tried to throw the same punch. "Like that?"

"Yup, just like that," catching my punch. "That punch right there will make a ngh swallow and spit at the same damn time."

Unc can fight anybody, whoop anybody's ass . . . except for dynamite. Dynamite is crack and heroin mixed up—it's undefeated.

"You clean?" my mom asked him on the phone the other day. I was eavesdropping on the other phone.

"Seven months. Think about using every day, but I'm clean. Intend on staying that way too." Before they hung up, he said, "Send the boy. I'll get him in line."

Uzi's going through his dresser. It's got so much graffiti on it I can't tell the original color. It's bombed out like one of the subway cars in the train yard near my grandma's house on Grand Concourse in the Bronx.

Top drawer—

"Want these?" he asks, tossing nunchucks at me.

"Yeah!" I catch, swing. They're really just two wooden paper towel holders chained together.

"Take these too." He throws brass knuckles at me. I slide my fingers into the four holes that look like the Audi rings. Make a fist.

"And yo—don't get caught with none of this shit either," Uzi tells me. I nod like a bobblehead and throw a brass jab at the air. "I'm not tryna hear Mom's mouth."

Middle drawer—

Black and silver Krylon spray paint and a couple of fat cap nozzles.

Bottom drawer—

A Phillies Blunt box full of sticky photos. He hands me this pic of a naked jawn. "What you know about that, Malo?"

"Damn," I say. "Her titties look like two bald heads." Uzi laughs and hands me another photo.

"'Member this?" It's a hazy pic of me and Uzi.

"Nah," I say. "When was this?"

"That's from when we moved here. Our first day in Philly. Mom took this," he says. I keep staring at the photo.

"I look shook."

"You were! You don't remember that day? You don't remember what you asked me when we were watching the fire?"

I shake my head nah. "What fire?"

"That was the day they bombed MOVE."

"Who bombed who?"

"Mayor Goode had the police drop a bomb on this group called MOVE, right there on Osage Avenue. We could see the blaze from our building."

"Oh yeah," I say slow, remembering, seeing the smoke curl behind my eyes. "That was a bomb?"

"Yeah, they dropped C-4 with Tovex on the whole block. That's the shit NASA uses to blow up asteroids and whatnot. Mad people died—women, kids. Shit was crazy. Mom is friends with one of the survivors—Ramona Africa."

"So what did I ask?"

"We were watching it go down—the smoke, the helicopters, sirens—you asked me if it was the end of the world." We both laugh. "It was, though, in a way. It was the end of the world we knew. We moved into a burning city."

He pulls one last thing out of his dresser: a deck of cards. He shuffles them, then they disappear, and reappear in my pocket. I'm like, "What the . . . ?" and he's just flashing this crazy grin.

"See, Malo, every ngh knows magic—look how we disappear when five-o rolls up." I laugh, thinking, *And reappear in jail?* "For real, though, magic is all about misdirection. Large movements to cover small movements. And every magician needs a signature trick."

I wish I knew magic. My signature trick would be to make the cops—the ones that stormed through our door that day, then into my dreams most nights like a horrible movie playing over and over in my head—disappear. Poof. Be gone.

I hug Uzi tight and try not to let go. I feel like if I let him go, he'll be gone forever. I can't fight back the tears. If he comes back tomorrow, it'll be too long.

3

10 Gs

I wake up in Uzi's room. Kool G Rap, Big Daddy Kane, the Fat Boys, Rob Base, Eric B and Rakim, Cool C, NWA, the Ultramagnetic MCs, Crown Rulers, PE, Wu-Tang, and like three years' worth of *Jet* magazine Beauties of the Week watching over me. Dimes in bikinis and baby oil. *Lashonda Harrington is from Abilene, TX. She enjoys scuba diving, reading, and cooking. Shanika Frazier is from Dayton, OH. The 5'5" model enjoys exercising, shopping, and dancing. Kia Dawson is from Trenton, NJ. She plans to study business administration and communications. Kimberly Jackson is an aspiring songwriter who resides in Texas. She enjoys playing dominoes and watching football. Malo enjoys them all.*

Uzi's gone, but I can still hear him singing, "Wake up, wake up, wake up, wake up," over my bed in his Bone Thugs-N-Harmony voice. When he was here, we'd walk to Broad and Olney together to go to school, cracking jokes and laughing the whole way. He'd hop on the C or the 55, whichever came first, and I'd get on the sub, the Orange Line. Now it's just me, solo-dolo. I feel naked without him.

I walk up to the corner of 10th and Godfrey—we call it 10 Gs—where all of Uzi's boys chill. They stand where they always stand, between the liquor store and the corner store, next to the Fern Rock Apartments fence, under the train tracks, and across the street from Rock Steady, this bugged ngh who sits on a crate all day with a broken radio, rocking his head back and forth to a beat no one else can hear. My mom calls them the "corner boys" because they're always out there, posted like guards at a checkpoint. They hug the block, huddled in hustle, eyeing everything and everyone everywhere every day.

She says: "They're bringing down the neighborhood . . . They're looking for trouble . . . They're an eyesore."

I just say: "Waddup?"

All the usual suspects are here: Ted, Scoop, D-Rock, and AB—the squad.

" 'Sup, young buck?" Scoop rumbles, shaking my hand like he's trying to prove a point, squeezing the red out. My hand feels like a Juicy Juice carton.

"Damn, man," I say, shaking the sting out.

"Yeah! You feel that shit, ngh?" He laughs his wicked laugh like he's possessed or something. "I break, not shake. I crush, not brush. Bruise, not cruise."

"Y'all up early?" I say, since I know none of them are in school. I think they'd be seniors like Uzi. They all dropped out around the same time. Ted always says he graduated valedictorian from the school of hard knocks.

9 6 the deal, we real about this cheddar, forever
Corner standing, in any weather*

"Up early? Nah, you up early. We ain't been to sleep yet. We up late."

"Sleep is the cousin of death," D-Rock says.

"Speaking of cousins," Scoop says, his sharp face behind a Newport, "you talk to Kiki?" Scoop is skinny with a face the color of unfinished wood. Cartoon eyes sunk low in sleepy sockets. Long dangly arms. A meaty W. C. Fields nose that's always red at the tip like Rudolph's. He's got the kind of hair that can go to the Puerto Rican, black, or white-boy barbershops, the shape-up curly top with gel. He's wearing all Polo—his outfit looks like a horse stable.

"Nah."

Takes a drag. "She still mad?"

"She's always mad at ya black ass," Ted says.

"Fuck you, Theodore." Scoop and Ted are always talking shit to each other, it's how they show love.

Kianna—Kiki—is my older cousin and Scoop's girl. This time she's mad at him because he beat up these two guys her first day at college. She goes to Albright in Reading, up there with all the name-brand outlets and the Puerto Rican gangs.

We helped her move into her dorm, me and Scoop, carry-

* "Illegal Life," Capone-N-Noreaga, 1996.

ing all her stuff up three flights of stairs. After that we found the gym on campus. It's nice, state-of-the-art everything. We were playing basketball against these two dudes—"college nghz," Scoop kept calling them, like it's a diss. I don't even know what homie said, but he said something, and Scoop just went off. Dropped dude with a right hook to the jaw. Then he rushed my guy like a gust of wind—strangled him. I was just standing there shell-shocked at the three-point line, like, *What the fuck, Scoop?*

We left right before the cops came. The school put Kianna on some kind of probation.

"I can't take him anywhere," she whines to me on the phone. "He's too niggerish. I'm getting too old for this shit." I remember when all that thug shit turned her on. "It's not cute anymore," she says. "I'm in college now."

I'll never forget the first day I met Scoop: "Why they call you Scoop?" I asked.

"Cuz I be scooping nghz' chins with uppercuts!" he said in his Badlands rasp. He's from the Badlands, 3rd and Cambria. His voice is ill because no one sounds like him. It's like he has a rattly muffler in his throat. His tone can flip from vicious to hilarious to straight cryptic in a blink.

I fucked with those beyond my age bracket
cuz they analyze and mack to get the papers and stack it*

A hooptie skids in the middle of the street. Some lady I see around sometimes, older, always in scrubs, rolls down the window. Shakes her head.

* "Gimme Yours," AZ, 1995.

“Damn, y’all *still* out here?” she jokes.

Ted jumps up, strikes a pose, and sings “Always and Forever” like Heatwave.

“Yo, Malo, why your peoples ship your big brother away like that?” Ted asks.

“I can’t even call it.” I step to school.

4

Friends or Foes?

My school colors are piss yellow and shit brown. The building is the color of shit too, like someone took a monster dump and smeared it all over.

This kid Fritz, my boy Ryan's cousin, actually did that last year on Mischief Night, the night before Halloween. Me and the squad went out mobbing around Olney, throwing eggs at cars, buses, people, whatever, it's a Philly tradition. We doused this abandoned U-Haul truck, Florida plates, with kerosene Ryan found in his uncle's basement. Nobody wanted to light it . . . *fuck it, I'll do it*. I swiped the match, stared long and hard into its glow until the flame crept down, pinching my fingertips, then threw it in. The fire jumped up like hibachi, scorching my leg. We ran up 7th Street as the truck blew up. After that, Fritz, who I've never liked and is known for taking shit a hundred miles too far, decided to literally take shit too far. We all told him not to do it but he was hell-bent. He took a shit in the bushes, scooped it up with the *Philadelphia Daily*

News, and smeared it on somebody's front door—the wrong somebody. Nasty. That somebody, a stocky old head who was in the Gulf War, caught Fritz and it was lights out. Fritz gets what he deserves, what's coming to him. Dude beat his ass with a Louisville Slugger. Then he made Fritz eat it . . . his own shit.

That's what going to a Friends school is like—eating your own shit. And inside Principal Roach's office, where I am now, is even worse than eating your own shit—it's eating someone else's. Roach limps around all day yelling at me about rules. He's got that rare type of limp that, once you meet him, you feel like he deserves.

I don't even know why I'm here or what I did. My teacher just sent me here as soon as I walked in. Roach's office is small and messy. Greasy thumbprints smudge all his scattered papers like drunk watermarks. I'm sitting here, waiting for him, thinking how I'd rather scrape dry blood off the sidewalk than be here waiting for him.

I wonder what Uzi is up to. What he's doing right now? I wish I was in the desert with him. I got a letter from him the other day:

Malo,

Wassup kid? Damn it's been a minute since we spoke yo. Uncle Jabbar kicked me out. Fuck him, he's a hater . . . He's jealous or some shit. He's tryna b my pop but I don't have a pop. My journey = my pop. My mistakes = my beatings. My personal triumphs = my pat on the head.

I'm good though, I always got a chick or two or five to lay up wit for a day or so, then on to the next. I wish u could be out here man, u should see this shit, a Philly ngh in AZ, doin rap shows, smuttin these coke-snortin Beckys and Suzies in their $2000 a month trust fund baby condo flop houses—shit is wild, just stay there for like a week partying, binging, it's nuts.

I hit Moms up for money sometimes, she'll send a couple dollars Western Union. I don't even really need the shit, I think I do it out of spite, like fuck it, u want me to stay away? Then pay!

My new crew is N.A.M. / New Age Militia / Nubian Apocalyptic Military / Niggaz Anglos and Mexicans / Nines and Macs / Narcotics and Money, u know! We just b partying, getting money, rumblin, gettin into all types of shit but overall just havin a good ass time in this short ass life we got dog.

Arizona is a gun state so u can buy ratchets at the pawn shop yo! Everybody's strapped! I like carrying my AP-9, it's like a newer version of the bum ass TEC-9, jawn is vicious . . . Get down or lay down! I'm not trying to hurt nobody, Malo, but these nghz out here b trippin, they gangbang and shit, I gotta protect my self cuz I'm all I got!

I'm still out here alone tho, I feel like an orphan, it seems like all my boys come from some kind of mysterious background . . . no family, no roots, I'm a Nomadic Addict Merchant (N.A.M.) . . . that's why we call ourselves a fam, a band of brothers.

And for real, Malo, I'm in no rush to come home. I want

to see u, be around u, but other than that, I might not ever come back . . . I'm finally free yo! I don't have to live up to my parents, my potential, nothin . . . does that sound fucked up? It's not. Look at all the 1st-round draft picks in the NFL or NBA that turned into bust, u know why?

Expectation before acclimation . . . Tryin to live up to some shit they wasn't even comfortable wit yet . . . Yahmean?

Look, man, take care of Mom, I know she is probably going through it. She's a quiet screamer, she won't tell me what the real deal is, so just look out for her. Play all the leeches in her life close, make them uncomfortable. Make sure Dad treats u with respect, and if he don't, show him none, none! . . . N.A.M.! (New Asante Men!)

My parents send me to this school because it's supposed to be better than the neighborhood schools in Olney that most of my boys go to. Better how? All we do is memorize stuff and spit it back like robots. It's called Friends, but it should be called Foes. They act one way to your face, but behind closed doors it's another story. Like how someone wrote *nigger* inside my locker when I was suspended. I have no idea who did it because nobody acts the part. I write back in my locker: *Say it to my face, bitch!*

It's like my pops says about racists from the North vs. the South: "I like my racism the way I like my whiskey—straight up," even though he doesn't really drink. "Down South they just come right out and call you a nigger, tell you they don't want anything to do with you, and at least you know where you stand . . . and where they stand. But up North, hunh . . ." His blood boils when he talks about racism. "Up here they pretend to be liberal but are some of the most racist white folks you'll ever meet in your life."

Word is bond. I like how Pops is always standing up for black people, how he don't take no shit.

One day my basketball coach, Coach Z, pulls me to the side during practice.

"What's up with you and the principal?" he asks. I shrug. *He doesn't fuck with me. I don't fuck with him. Nothing new.* "Be careful." He lowers his tone. "I was getting some coffee in the teachers' lounge and I overheard him say he hates you."

"Hates me?"

I didn't see that coming. Not the hate. The pain. Hates me? It feels like a punch in the gut. Coach searches my eyes.

"Fuck him. I hate him too."

"Look, I know he's a jerk. But be careful, he's got it out for ya. I need you on my team come state tournament time. This is our year to win the division."

I'm in eighth grade but I play on the high school varsity team. Coach is always looking out for me. He gives me a key to the gym. Tells me I can play ball during class. He says I'm the best player in the league.

"If it weren't for me, you'd be long gone," he always says. He looks out for me, but I know it's only because I can dribble, dish, and dunk.

Roach's hate for me started a while ago at Meeting for Worship. MFW is when you sit in silence in a big hollow room on these cold wooden benches. It's like church but with no preacher, no Bibles, no music, no emotion, no nothing, just hard silence. You just sit there smelling stinkers and listening to yourself swallow.

The only break in silence is when someone feels moved enough to stand up and say something. No one ever does, except this one girl, Rachel, who just sucks up.

"I like this school because it's nice . . ."

"I like this school because the teachers are good . . ."

"I like this school because . . ."

Are you fucking serious?

So I responded one day. They say MFW is a time to let your voice be heard in the community, a time to share, a time to reflect on the school and what it means to you. I kept it real:

"I don't like this school because this school don't like me."

My friends—Avi, Naeemah, Crystal, and Jesse—shoved their knuckles in their mouth, trying to choke back the crack-up. They couldn't! Laughter gushed like fire hydrant water in the summer.

"Shushhh," the teachers sprayed like spitting insects.

After that Roach said I can't speak at MFW anymore. They want me to be silent. Silence is for dead people—I'm alive. Silence is betrayal to your thoughts—I'm thinking. I feel like screaming at the top of my lungs, so loud my ears pop like those little red M-80s from Chinatown that me and Uzi used to set off on July 4th.

—

My dad gets mad pissed at us for lighting fireworks on the Fourth. Not 'cause they can turn our fingers into knobs but because he doesn't fuck with July 4th or Christmas or Easter or Presidents' Day or any other holiday. Too white for Pops—white Christmas, all white on Easter, dead white presidents. He comes outside.

"Whose independence are you celebrating?" He pulls out a book and reads while the M-80 smoke swirls over our heads: "'What, to the American slave, is your Fourth of July? I answer: a day that reveals to him, more than all other days in the year, the gross injustice and cruelty to which he is the constant victim. To him, your celebration is a sham; your boasted liberty, an unholy license; your national greatness, swelling vanity; your sounds of rejoicing are empty and heartless; your denunciation of tyrants, brass-fronted impudence; your shouts of liberty and equality, hollow mockery; your prayers and hymns, your sermons and thanksgivings, with all your religious parade and solemnity, are, to him, mere bombast, fraud, deception, impiety, and hypocrisy—a thin veil to cover up crimes which would disgrace a nation of savages.'"

Roach tried to put me on meds: Ritalin, Adderall, Dexedrine, whatever.

"They are crazy if they think I'm going to let them give you Ritalin or whatever," Mom said. "You're just a boy. Boys are boys and will be boys."

I asked my parents to send me to the public school.

"We make a lot of sacrifices to send you to a good school," my parents said. "We can't afford it but we find a way." My dad told me how their parents, my grandparents, never made it past second grade and how black people need school like fish need water. How him and my mom were the first ones in their families to ever graduate from high school.

So I'm at this school for everyone in my family and all the black people who never got a chance to sit here. I know who I'm here for, but I still don't know why I'm here in Roach's office.

Finally he huffs in, mumbling something. Pushes the door shut. I know he wants to slam it, but he's too puss.

"What's your problem with authority?" he asks, gasping for air like he just ran a marathon even though all he did was plop down. He's so fat he runs out of breath trying to catch his breath.

"What is it, huh?" His breath smells like burnt mayonnaise and spoiled scrapple on rotten rye. "What's your problem with authority?" He's got old food crumbs stuck in his red beard that look like little insect eggs in a crusty nest. I try not to look, try to look at something else. I see a poster of Elvis that says *The King Lives On* and keep looking.

"What's your problem with me?" I say.

"Well, let's see," he says, making a church steeple with his fingers, then looking me up and down. "For starters, look at you." I'm wearing jeans, Timbs, a red Phillies fitted hat, a white tee with a Tommy Hilfiger breakaway—fresh like Dougie. Him, on the other hand . . . He needs to dust-bust his face. He needs a redo. His clothes are filthy, so dirty I can see the dirt on the inside from the outside like dead bugs in a lamp shade.

"Look at me," I say.

"Where do you think you are? This is Friends—"

"Foes!"

"—not North Philly," he says. I laugh. "Your personality and attitude are unacceptable."

In the South, blacks can get close as long as they don't get uppity. I remember my dad's words. *In the North, blacks can get uppity as long as they don't get close.*

"My personality is who I am. My attitude depends on who you are."

"What is your problem with the rules?" Roach asks.

"What rules? I don't even know why I'm here, man."

"Well, let's see." He laughs. "Which ones did you break today?" He writes something down. He's always jotting notes on me.

"Your paper trail is growing." He raises his notebook to his beady eyes.

"Take off your hat," he says.

A few months ago my grandfather died. I didn't know him that well, but I spent time with him in Valdosta, Georgia, before he passed. He was paralyzed from the waist down from an accident he had working on the Georgia Pacific Railway.

Loved sports, told me about Joe Louis whupping Max Schmeling's ass, about Jesse Owens winning four medals in front of Hitler.

He tells me, "Don't take yo hat off fo nobody . . . 'less you want to."

"No," I tell Roach, looking him right in the eyes.

"Off!"

"Why?"

"Because it's against the rules," he screams. That line right there—*because it's against the rules*—is the number one sign of a bullshit rule. I pull my hat down even tighter, crank it hard to the side.

"Do you know what happens to people who can't follow rules?"

I'm over this. "There should be a rule against your breath . . ."

"You're skating on thin ice," he shouts like we're in the army.

"You shouldn't be allowed to—"

"Thin ice!" He flashes his fangs. His teeth, like little rusty corkscrews, threatening. "I'm calling your parents!"

My face says every curse word to him.

"Stay put," he says, and huffs out.

When he's gone, I stand up and gaze out of the tall, thin window in his office. From here I can see Love Park. I can see the Valentine-red letters—thick and stacked like building blocks—that spell *LOVE* in the center of the action. Love is the mecca for street skateboarding. Skaters from all over the world come to Philly just to skate the marble ledges, fountains, and stairs of Love. Being down the street from it is the best thing about my school.

Some days after school, or even during, me and my best friend, Amir, grab our boards and hit Love. Amir is tall and skinny with skin the color of my mom's coffee—black, one cream, no sugar—and big, bright eyes shaped like sideways teardrops. We met playing ball at Fisher Park a couple of years ago and have been tight ever since. We chill even more these days because Uzi's in Arizona. We eat together, share gear, and even holla at the same girls. We tell them we're cousins. On the weekends we steal my mom's car and hit up one of the under-twenty-one clubs like Dancers or Gotham. We always make it back uptown right before the sun comes up and my mom wakes up.

At Love, we skate and chill and joke and watch lil' Stevie—this young buck with big lips and electric Ol' Dirty Bastard hair—push through Love, riding, cruising, ollieing over trash cans clean, kick-flipping into ledges, grinding, spinning, catching wreck, arms dangling like empty shirtsleeves, landing sick trick after sick trick like it ain't shit. Stevie's so good he makes the suits cutting through the park on their lunch breaks stand speechless while their food gets cold. So good he makes the bums who sleep the days away on the benches wake up and clap.

The cops who patrol the park remind me of Roach. Every day they storm Love—scuffed nightsticks clenched above their heads like flagpoles—chasing us into 15th Street traffic. They say we can't skate Love even though it's public.

Fuck tha police comin straight from the underground

Young ngh got it bad cuz I'm brown*

"This is the Philadelphia Police . . . leave the park immediately, leave the area immediately," they yell over the bullhorn. If they catch somebody, they'll break their board and take them to the station. Me and Amir never get caught, though. We see the paddy wagons as soon as they roll up and yell, "Jakes!"

Roach comes back with an index card with my last name on it and a whole bunch of notes and cross-outs. He lifts the horn and starts dialing . . .

"I'm having a difficult time trying to reach your parents." His ear is to the phone and he's shaking his head.

Join the club.

"Where's your dad?"

"I don't know." I never know where my dad is these days, just that he's always gone. When he's not gone, he's getting gone.

"He's a busy man," I tell Roach. But no matter how mad I get at Pops for being gone all the time, as soon as I see him, I'm happy again, whole, like he never left.

"So I hear," Roach says. "I saw his interview on *60 Minutes*." I think about it—that was probably the last time I saw my pops too, on TV. I remember watching him tell the interviewer: "I can honestly say that I have never found a school

* "Fuck tha Police," N.W.A, 1988.

in the United States run by whites that adequately prepares black children to enter the world as sane human beings." *So what the hell am I doing here in this white-ass school then?* Roach is glaring at me, probably wondering the same thing.

"What about your older sister?" he says.

I shrug. My sister is in a mental hospital. She sees and hears things we can't.

She came to stay a weekend with us a while back.

"Be nice to your sister," my dad told me before she arrived, not knowing what else to say. She lives with her mom in Anaheim, California. She's a pretty girl with dark, glass-smooth skin. Her favorite hobby is family genealogy.

"We have a direct lineage from a king of Wales and a direct lineage to the Earl of Sunderland. We're related to some other famous celebrities like actresses Lucille Ball and Carole Lombard; actor Vincent Leonard Price; first president of the American Red Cross, Clara Barton; forties sex symbol Rita Hayworth; actress Raquel Welch; and also the first president of Harvard, Henry Dunster."

I was sitting with her on the bed in my room, smiling at her imagination. She kept going: "We're Irish, Welsh, Hawaiian, Native American, German, French Canadian, Scottish, Spanish, Seminole Indian, Creole, Cherokee, Sioux Indian, Shawnee Indian, and Flamenco Gypsy from Madrid Spain."

Later on she told my pops about her genealogy research. He got heated: "Anika, we are African. African American. Black."

She whispered to me, "Dad's African royalty is adopted African royalty because he went to Africa and became a king and that's how he got his African royalty." This whole scene is wild to me—how the daughter of the father of Afrocentricity claims to be whiter than snow. Every day Anika sees these people she calls the "neighbors."

"What they look like?"

"They're white . . . they called me a 'black bitch.' They said, 'Kill that black bitch,' and pointed at me. 'Let's hang blackie from the tree. She doesn't belong here. We're gonna kill you. We're coming to get you, black bitch.' " The meds make her eyes sandstorm hazy, slur her speech.

I said, "Tell them to kiss the darkest part of your black ass." She chuckled through the pill fog. My sis makes me think seeing isn't always believing and believing isn't always seeing.

She went back to Cali and sent me a letter a couple of months later:

Hi Malo,

How are you? Anaheim is okay but I still want to move out of California. The people in California are very mean to me and the police are everywhere and the KKK and the racists are all harassing me and threatening me and they want to take me to jail and kill me . . . and I'm mixed! So this is going to be a very depressing and not good summer! But when it's not summer I feel happy, not scared and depressed! But what's really hurtful is that Mom and Dad don't believe me about the police and racists are after me in California trying to kill me and put me in jail or a mental institution or hospital!! :-(And I didn't do anything. I'm innocent! I definitely don't want to go to jail because jail is the end of the world! And they would keep me there till the end of time. So pray for me! Nobody believes me. Mom and Dad don't believe me. Well just wait until they see what I do to them! Ha-ha.

Tomorrow I'll call a place I saw on TV for my inventions. I invent things or just think of inventions. Anyway pray that they go well.

I've still been doing our genealogy! I found out on my mom's side not only do I have English and Welsh royalty, I have French royalty too! Told Dad too! I'm related to the Earl of Sydney (1055–1088). His name was William de Wanenne. And we're from the Wanenne family who settled in New England in the early 1600s. As well as being related to Eli Whitney, inventor of the cotton gin, and President Ulysses S. Grant. Isn't that cool? I think it's way cool!

On Dad's side we're Spanish and Irish, from the Wilkins family, and we're related to Hernando de Soto. We're also related to the Kennedys from Boston. What a shocker! But I'm happy that I'm Irish.

Well, gotta go, bye!

P.S. The KKK bring their dogs down my street so that they can bite me on purpose. I gotta get out of the USA and move to another country, and I gotta get out before I get bitten and die. They don't want to see me rich either.

P.S.S. The reason why my mom doesn't believe me is because her mom didn't believe her!

"My sister's not around," is all I tell Roach. That's the most he deserves.

"And what about your mom?" He already knows where she is. The other day my dad got in touch with my school and told them what's going on. Now he's playing dumb, trying to embarrass me.

"Where is she, huh? Where's your mom?"

"Fuck you," I say, looking forward to suspension.

5

Open Secrets

They steal my mom away on the same day Tupac dies. It's the middle of the night when I hear the back door slam hard. I look out the window. I can't believe he's dead. The greatest rapper ever, dead at twenty-five. Midnight downpour. I watch the lines of rain streak across the angelic glow of street lights. Flecks of rain dot the window.

My mom is wearing the flowy cream nightgown she sleeps in. My dad eases her into the passenger seat of his two-door Nissan and sprints around to the driver's side. The headlights pop up like goggles and the coupe skids off into the wet night.

I heard a rumor I died, murdered in cold blood dramatized
Pictures of me in my final stages, you know mama cried*

* "Ain't Hard to Find," 2Pac, 1996.

The next morning, I see my dad on my way to school. He's got bags in both hands, on his way somewhere, someplace.

"Your mother's in the hospital."

"What's wrong with her?"

"She's . . . sick."

"Well, can I see her?"

"Not yet."

"How long is she going to be there for?"

"I don't know. Until she gets better."

"But what's wrong with her? Like exactly?"

"It's up here," he says, fingering his temple, "and right here," touching his heart.

"What hospital?"

"One you've never heard of," he says. He tells me that he has to bounce for a few days and that my cousin Kianna is coming to stay with me. Then he gives me the phone number to the hospital.

I call . . . "Philadelphia Psychiatric Center." I hang up—*fuck*.

Kianna tells me that my mom tried to kill herself.

And through all the motherfuckin pain
They done drove my moms in-sane*

When my dad is gone, I snoop through their room. I pull out his double-barreled shotgun. Load it. Feels way heavier

* "Streiht Up Menace," MC Eiht, 1993.

loaded. In the mirror hanging on the closest door, I point the 12-gauge right at my face. I wonder what would happen if I pulled the trigger? If I killed my reflection?

I move to my mom's stuff, find her journal.

I think about how much I love her, but how we don't really speak. I come in when I come in. She's in her chair with the TV on, watching *Cops* or *Murder, She Wrote,* with her pills and her water and empty ice cream containers and folded newspapers. She reads four newspapers every day: *Philadelphia Inquirer, Philadelphia Daily News, Philadelphia Tribune*, and *New York Times*.

The journal is heavy to be so little. Does ink weigh that much? Can ink weigh that much?

"Letters to Carole" is written on the cover. Carole was her name before Amina.

I open it and see names everywhere: mine, my dad's, Uzi's. My heart speeds and sinks. I close it fast, scared of what it might say.

I want to open it again. I know it's wrong, I know I shouldn't, but I have to. She never tells me what's up with her, so now the matter's in my hands. Maybe this is our chance, my chance . . . I open it and hear my mom's voice for the first time in a long time: *My first attempt at suicide was at twelve. I tried to overdose . . . My scars are symbols of a terrible beauty that speaks to life . . . Malo will leave soon, like I did, and never come back . . .*

These are her private thoughts. Close it. I miss her voice, though. Miss her.

Open . . .

Dear Carole,

I never took drugs even though they were all around me. I don't really count smoking weed as a drug but Bob was a heroin addict and my brother, Jabbar, has been a crack addict on and off, so I know drugs. But the drugs prescribed for my depression are a different story. They serve the same purpose as crack or heroin, a way of escaping, of turning away from the pain and an excuse to leave the planet momentarily. My drugs are legal but the result, the high, feels the same. It doesn't make much sense to me that a doctor could know what medicine to give someone for depression anyway. Depression is so specific, so historical and so particular, how could a pill deal with all that? The pills don't deal with any of that.

All they do is make the time go by dulling my senses and making me sleep. Taking my meds is like putting a sign on my door that says *Unavailable*. It works. The only person to ignore the sign is Malo. At least when he was younger, he ignored the sign, but now, as a teenager, he keeps his distance and tells other people, "Mom don't feel well." Malo is staring at a woman who doesn't seem herself. It's not that I'm not myself, but I have buried myself so that I don't feel any pain. Daudi doesn't get it and it makes him angry. Malo accepts it even if he doesn't get it. I'm in my bedroom, either in bed or in my chair, but always out of commission. I'm in a fog and I prefer it that way.

There are moments when I can function but the point is I don't want to function. I want no part of this life. The pills aid my escape. Sometimes I take more than I'm supposed to.

No one knows what I'm taking, just the doctor. I keep stockpiles, always making allowances for that day when I might need to permanently "leave." "Leaving" has been on my mind most of my life. My first attempt at suicide was at twelve. I tried to overdose on aspirins. I was eighteen when I tried again. I took an overdose of pills. I was hospitalized. I didn't tell my family. So now I have my stash just in case I need to permanently check out.

Chaka believes that medicine can cure anything, I know better. He's always so encouraged every time the doctor prescribes a new medicine. "This will work" is his mantra, and so off I go into another world until I tire of the charade and stop taking the medication. It isn't that the medication doesn't work, but it doesn't work the way that Chaka wants it to work. It doesn't work the way that I want it to work. He wants magic, a pill that can make me new again. But just like me, that pill doesn't exist.

Sitting in my chair in my bedroom, the world comes and goes. Malo comes and goes, often without stopping by my bedroom or saying a word. Chaka comes and goes, making sure he leaves in the morning when I'm asleep and comes home so late at night when I'm sure to be asleep. What he doesn't know is that I'm not asleep. Knowing that he wants me to be asleep, I pretend to be asleep. It makes things easier for both of us.

If my family knows that I'm on medication, they don't say anything. The only thing that they know is that I don't come up to the Bronx anymore or talk to anyone. There is no intervention, nor does anyone say, "What the hell is going on?" That would be comforting. It would mean that someone is looking out for me, willing to stand up for me and perhaps even go to bat for me. Who do I go to when I'm tired or needy? I can nuzzle my face in Malo's chest, and that always makes me feel a little better, but I can't talk to him. I can't talk to Chaka unless it's about Afrocentricity or The Movement or telling him I'm getting better.

What does "better" mean, anyway? Does it mean healed? Does it mean changed? Better doesn't mean anything, and if better came through the door, no one would recognize it—and worse, it would be unwelcome.

The escape I yearn for is real. I want to escape the harsh upbringing of my childhood and a mother who blamed me for our poverty. I want to escape a husband who promised to take care of me and instead I was taking care of him. I want to escape a world that seemed to have broken every promise made in my dreams.

God, give me strength.

Amina

6

Ginga

I'm at Broad and Olney, the station where I catch the bus and the sub, after school with Amir and my two other boys, Kam and Ryan. We're posted up in front of Mickey D's, thumbs in backpack straps, inhaling the scene. I'm cracking up because Amir and Ryan are busting on each other, tit for tat.

"Ya mom so stupid it took her five hours to watch *60 Minutes*."

"Ya mom so short she poses for trophies."

We bust on each other because we fucks with each other, 'cause we love each other. It's just like how Joey Merlino and the Italian mob in South Philly slap each other's faces—La Cosa Nostra, crew love. Amir is the reigning bust champion, he's slap-your-thighs-tilt-ya-head-back-make-ya-stomach-hurt funny.

Kam puts his hands up to me and we slap-box. I catch him, he catches me, our hands flicking out fast at each other like snake tongues.

Broad and Olney has everything and everybody happening at the same time.

"Ya mom so dumb she thought a quarterback was a refund."

"Ya mom so dumb she thought St. Ides was a church."

You got the Hebrew Israelites on soapboxes with bullhorns, dressed like low-budget pharaohs, Bibles flapping in the wind like flags, screaming about how the original Jews are blacks and disciples and prophets and whatever.

"Ya mom feet so big her sneaks need license plates."

"Ya mom so stupid I told her it was chilly outside . . . she grabbed a spoon."

The hack cab guys—old heads with windbreakers and Kangols and canes and chew sticks—posted up, saying "Hack cab, hack cab, hack cab" to everyone that walks by. The people at the top of the escalator passing out flyers and pamphlets to anybody who'll take one.

"Ya mom so fat she sweat gravy."

"Ya mom so fat she got baptized at Sea World."

The tired sighs of Septa buses, here, there, all around, braking and letting people out—*pshhhhhh*. Music floating from the cars stopped at the light, from the urban wear spots with their iron-bar doors opening and closing, from this lady with the headphones who just got off work humming to Keith Sweat, and from the music already in my head.

"Ya mom so black she sweat Pepsi . . . She fart smoke . . . She go to funerals naked . . . Lightning bugs follow her during the day."

"Ya mom so black she sweat Yoo-hoo . . . She pee coffee . . . She bleed oil . . . She goes to night school and gets marked absent."

The hustlemans trying to sell everything, anything: black soap, white tees, incense, bootleg movies, weed, kufis, socks, watches and sunglasses from China, noni juice, Omar Tyree paperbacks, bean pies, pretzels, body oils, whatever moves, whatever flips. Dirty fat pigeons flapping above us all.

And B & O is full of girls, jawns. Our game is to see who can pull the most numbers. Girls gloss by. I love them all. Each girl, like her own planet, with her own orbit, moon, sun, rotation. Sometimes they throw me a little rhythm. Gravitational pull.

"Would you hit it?" Amir asks, pointing with his head. She's got on skintight Guess jeans and a leather bomber. From the side, her ass looks like a capital *C*.

"Dayum," Ryan says as she walks by, "I'd tear it up."

"Excuse me? Tear what up?" She stops, spins. Ryan just stands there, shook. "You wouldn't know what to do with this, little boy," she cracks, sizing him up, laughing as she swishes away. We all bust out laughing.

"Little boy? I got your little boy, all right. Got your little boy right here," he yells, grabbing his sack. But he knows she can't hear him or see him.

"She played you," I say.

"Man, I'd have that jawn screaming my name, calling me daddy and everything."

"Oh yeah?"

"Fucking real." He faces the wall and acts like he's fucking her against it. He folds his arms and lets his fingers crawl up his back as if they were hers. "Have her like, 'Oooh, ah, oooh, papi chulo, give me that big dick, this is your pussy, daddy.' "

"Look, look, look," Kam says under his breath, pointing where I'm already looking.

I spot her getting off the bus. Her skin glitters in the after-school sun. Gentle eyes—I catch them.

"Holla at her." He nudges me.

"Who, her?" I say like I can't see her. But she's all I see.

"Yeah . . . with the uniform."

Her face is soft, round and golden like my grandma's pancakes. I glance down at my sneaks. Jawns always peep your footwear first; Kianna taught me that. A few scuffs on my Timbs ain't stopping this train.

Feel the good vibrations

So many females, so much inspiration*

I'm learning how to talk to girls. There's an art to it. It's not about spitting some recycled lines. Philly girls hear the same lines all day like the chorus from a radio single:

Shawty, let me holla at you for a minute . . .
How you doin', baby? . . .
What's up with me and you, sweetheart? . . .
Let me get them digits, yo . . .
What's good, ma? . . . What's really good, ma? . . . What's really really good? . . .

* "93 'Til Infinity," Souls of Mischief, 1993.

I'm saying, though, I'm tryna see you like that . . .
Excuse me, miss. Let me whisper in your ear.

All that shit is dead. Getting girls is really about Ginga.

Ginga is what separates the Brazilians from the rest of the world in soccer. Uzi broke it down for me one day when we were watching *SportsCenter*. They were showing highlights of Brazil's team.

"Peep the way they play, peep their rhythm. That's Ginga! It's an attitude, a way of life, like soul, style, and swag all rolled into one. It's not just how you move, it's when you move, where you move, and why you move. Ging-ga! Nig-ga!"

When it comes to girls, you gotta have Ginga. Ginga gives you that bop in your step. Uzi told me: "Approach everything—the way you walk, talk, dance—with the right combination of toes, heels, and hips and you'll be in there like swimwear."

She floats down into the subway tunnel.

"Ging-ga," I say to myself as I jog down the stairs after her. As I approach, we catch eyes and suddenly I'm nervous.

"Hey, what's up," I say, my voice cracking like a piano. I can feel my homies peering from above, waiting to see if I'll be shot down.

"Hi . . . and bye," she says as the southbound Orange Line rumbles in. "This is my train." She swipes her TransPass and keeps moving.

I look up and see my boys laughing, pointing at me. I see the girl getting away, boarding the sub. *What if I never see her again?* I flash my homies the peace sign and hop the turnstile . . .

—

"This is my train too," I say, sitting next to her. "What's your name?"

"Nia. You?"

"Malo," I tell her as the train kicks, bucks, and clacks over the tracks.

"Malo?" she says, surprised. "I'm taking Spanish . . . You know what your name means in Spanish?"

"Nah, what?"

"Erie Avenue," the conductor's voice crackles through the speakers. "Erie Avenue."

My full name—Khumalo—means "prince" in Zulu. My parents changed their names back in the day.

"We didn't want slave names anymore," is how my dad explains it. "When black people came to America, we didn't have names like John and Bill and all that. They sold us like beasts, counting our teeth, feeling our testicles, testing the luster or dullness of our skin, changing our names, our religions, customs. Carrying the names of those who enslaved your ancestors is a constant reminder of a lack of self-determination, a badge of conquest. Having an English name and not looking like an English person plagued me most of my early life. I resented it since I can remember. Mature people give themselves names from their history and culture; others are like pets that are given names. We can name ourselves." So they went from Arthur Lee Smith and Carole Ann Welsh to Chaka and Amina Asante. And just like they chose their name, I choose mine—Malo.

"It means 'bad,'" she says. "Are you bad?" She laughs. I just look at her.

"Girard Avenue. Girard Avenue."

"Can I get your number?" I ask as the train screeches.

"Nope." My heart nose-dives into my stomach.

"Damn, it's like that?"

"I can't have boys call my house." A smile curls. "So give me yours."

"Paper?"

"Write it here," she says, and holds out her hand. I take her hand and kiss it with the Paper Mate. The ink doesn't show. Her hand feels soft and warm, like clothes fresh out of the dryer.

"It's not writing," I say, trying to form an *M* as the train slows.

"Press a little harder," she says. "It works. And you gotta hurry, this is my stop coming." I finish writing but don't want to let her hand go. She pulls away.

"Okay, I'll call you sometime."

"Spring Garden Street. Spring Garden Street."

"When?"

"Tonight," she says, running off the train.

Dear Carole,

Chaka's abandoning me and I've given up hope that he'll reflect on his role in abandoning the family even as he preaches about the black family. What is that? Why is that? The whole black community loves Chaka and they don't know the internal rhythms of pain and destruction that are happening in the family. I don't know either.

The house is quiet, expecting, and waiting. I can hear Chaka coming up the street and pulling into the driveway. He will come in and I will pretend to be asleep. He used to stop in Malo's room when he was little but he no longer does that. Just as well—Malo is not in his room. The quiet of the street belies the anxious stirring of teenage boys who are deep into their mischief. Malo is acting out in a secretive way.

I hear and see my car pull out of the driveway. Malo is on the prowl. He thinks that I don't know. I don't use my car every day but when I get into my car, I notice that things are different. Is this a rite of passage? I wouldn't know, as I didn't grow up with access to a car or even thought of driving. Maybe I'll say something to him in the morning. Malo may or may not admit to it but he won't apologize. This is a child who doesn't know how to say "I am sorry." What is that about? It's so interesting. He is an old soul in a young body. It is as if he has the right to do whatever is necessary and I am supposed to understand that. He loves to say, "Don't worry, Mom."

Where is he going? Is he seeing some girl? Is he hanging out with his friends? Is he drinking, drugging, or what? He will be home with the sunrise. I won't be awake when he drives back into the driveway. Is he running away from me? Did I run away from my mom? Well, I did, but in a different way. I was a difficult teenager, and like Malo, I felt as if my destiny was entirely in my hands. I "outgrew" my mother before I reached my teens. Malo will leave soon, like I did, and never come back.

My sister already caught Malo in his room with some girl that she called a "wench." I found nude photos of some girl in his room. Different girls call for him, LaTasha, Toya, Shanika, Alisha, too many to remember, at all hours of the night.

Everything is a secret. I am sure that he does this because he doesn't want to hurt me. It does hurt, but worse, it further divides Chaka and me. Chaka thinks that both boys' behavior points directly to me. He says I'm not strict enough and I give them too much. True, I am not strict and I probably have given them too much. But if it takes two to tango, then I am a solo dancer trying to raise two sons alone!

This is a house of secrets. Malo's nightly forays into the streets, Chaka's nightly forays at the office or out of town, and my nightly forays forgetting, escaping, and wishing pain away.

The house is quiet. My heart is racing. I want to touch Chaka and wake him. How is he doing, what is he thinking, what does he want? Can simple questions be that difficult? I am silent too; quiet! The night is still and I can hear Chaka's breathing (snoring). Daudi is away but I can hear his cry too. "Mom!" I can hear Malo's unspoken voice. He looks at me and proclaims; "I am a man. You won't have to worry about me like you worry about Uzi." Not true. Malo is my love child in more ways than one, but we don't talk.

My soul and heart are in flight. I am looking for me. I am looking for the "me" that I lost somewhere along the way. Morning has come. Malo is home, Chaka is up and I am pretending to be asleep. My oldest son is away and my home has become the house of secrets.

God, give me strength.

Amina

7

Phone Tap

The phone rings. Maybe it's Nia? My heart beats, rings with fear.

But as soon as I hear—

You have a collect call . . .

—I already know.

. . . from . . . "Uzi" . . . an inmate at the Arizona State Prison Complex . . . To accept this call press the star key—

* * * * * *

Your call is being connected.

"Hello?"

"Malo!"

"Uzi! What's up?"

"I fucked up, bro."

"What happened?"

"I got knocked. I'm in jail."

"For what?"

"Can't really talk about it right now, man, shit is crazy . . . put Mom on the phone."

"She's not here."

"Damn, where she at?" Uzi doesn't even know she's in the psych ward. Should I tell him?

"When you getting out?"

"I can't even call it, Malo."

"But you're a minor. Last time—"

"This ain't like last time. They tryna charge me as an adult."

A hollow silence.

You have ten seconds left for this call.

"I love you, man."

"Love you too."

"And yo, Malo?"

"Yeah?"

"Get me outta here!"

Dear Carole,

I took Daudi to the airport this morning. It was difficult. After all of the drama and situations, this tall skinny boy pleaded with me not to send him to Arizona. He is a baby inside and I had to be resolute. Only I wasn't. Was I doing the right thing? Daudi has been through his share of troubles with schools and run-ins with police, but why can't Chaka and I get a grip on things? Daudi is bright but seems to be unable to do well in school. Perhaps there was some kind of attention disorder. Now he is totally swept up in what his friends are doing, and unfortunately they're also up to no good.

Didn't black people always send their children to the South to give them some training or to get them straightened out? I'm following a tradition, or am I? Arizona isn't the South and my brother has problems of his own. This is a Hail Mary pass and even as I put Daudi on the plane I had my doubts. My brother has problems of his own. Right now he is sober but I don't know how long that will last.

Daudi looked so small in his long lanky body and his eyes glistened big and wet. What am I doing? Am I doing this to please Chaka? Truth be told, Daudi and Chaka never bonded. In the beginning it never occurred to me that he wouldn't love my son. He loved me and promised to take care of my son. I took him at his word. But it wouldn't be so easy. Chaka is not a child's person. He barks orders and expects little people to obey. He doesn't play or get down and dirty with children, so I guess that there was very little bonding for Daudi and him to do.

But I am Daudi's mother and I am responsible for him. He came into this world fighting and had an uphill battle healthwise. I remember saying to the doctor when I had to have surgery while he was still in my womb, "Please save my baby." He was so tiny when he arrived but he was fighting and I just knew that he would be this incredible child. I was right, but something happened.

I leave the airport feeling so sad. It is not a good day for me. In my heart, I know that I have let my son down. Am I doing this to lessen the stress in a house that is already filled with quiet tension? Am I doing this instead of doing something else, something more radical, like . . . what?

Malo will miss his brother. Will this make it better for Malo?

I am so full of doubt today when I should be more positive, but looking at Daudi walk down the hall to the plane reminded me when I put him in nursery school when he was three years old. It was in Buffalo and it was his first day. I dropped him off and he stood at the gate crying for me as I walked away. At least then, despite my aching heart, I knew that I would return to get him that evening. He isn't so sure now as I leave him; what is he thinking?

What am I thinking? I wish I could really talk to Chaka. But it is all pronouncements and sermons. He doesn't have time to really think about Daudi and doesn't give Malo any time either.

I can't dwell on this now but I want to go home and sleep for seven days and seven nights. I don't know how to deal with yet another pain. I want to scream while I dance and dance while I scream. I want to forget that pain can be so intimate. I want to travel beside Daudi on his collar, whispering in his ear, soothing his shoulders, kissing his cheeks, and telling him, "I love you."

If nothing else, I am a warrior. I must get stronger so I can be there for my sons. I have to resist going into a black hole and never seeing light. My strength is my light and both of my sons need me.

I can't say what the weather is like today or how the sky is tinged. All I can say is that I took Daudi to the airport to put him on a plane to Arizona. He cried, and as I walked away, the tears that were raining inside of me began to fill up the spaces in my eyes and then envelop my face until I couldn't see. I can't say how the weather is today but I know that inside me, it is raining.

God, give me strength.

Amina

8

Relapse

My mom's back from the hospital in the same nightgown she left in. She's in her chair, on the horn with my uncle, all the way reclined like she's at the dentist getting teeth pulled.

Outside is gusty, wind whirling through trees, leaves clapping. The wind slaps the house like it stole something. Slams the screen door into the jamb over and over again. Howls through the halls, haunting.

"He relapsed," she whispers to me, palming the mouthpiece. I sit on her bed and study her face: the winces, grimaces, and slow blinks. It's all a blur of bad news. The latest is that Uzi's in solitary confinement, so she can't speak to him. She hasn't talked to him yet. Uncle Jabbar has updates.

"Twenty-five years!" she cries out.

What the fuck? Twenty-five years of what?

I hear Uzi's voice over the prison static: *Get me outta here!*

"Oh God," Mom says. "What?" She can't stop shaking her

head. Weary lids. She tries to say something to me but can't get it out. She's melting right in front of me.

My mom's crying 'cause her insides are dyin
her son tryin her patience, keep her heart racin*

Later, I hear snatches of the story:

Uzi and his boy Antwan, they call him Shotgun, a Crip from St. Louis . . .

They fuck these girls from a group home, runaways . . .

She tells Uzi she's sixteen . . . she's thirteen . . .

And she's white.

* "Regrets," Jay-Z, 1996.

9

Neveruary

"I don't want you hanging on the corner," my mom says. "Those guys are too old for you anyway." I don't think they're too old, they're Uzi's age, but I don't argue with her about it. She's already mad stressed about Uzi, plus she just got back from the psych ward a few days ago. She's as delicate as eyelashes.

"'K, Ma . . . but I gotta walk past there to get home."

"You can go the other way."

"What other way?"

"The back way?"

"Up *Star Trek*?"

"Yes," she laughs, "and why do you call it that?"

"'Cause the baseheads, before they light up, say, 'Beam me up, Scotty.' They smoke crack out of car antennas."

"I just don't want you hanging on the corner. Just say hi and keep going. You don't have to stop for them."

"I got you."

"No, really," she says, sucking her teeth. "They are out there looking for young black boys to put in the system. I don't want you to become a statistic . . . like your brother."

"I got you."

"And what do you mean, you got me? I'm not your homie." She laughs.

"I won't hang down there."

But of course I do. What, I'm supposed to stay in the crib? The corner is popping, electric, buzzing. Anything can happen and does. Different people are always coming through and they all know Uzi and that I'm his little brother. And if they don't, once they find out—*oh, you Uzi's little bro?*—they show me mad love.

And momma told me, don't hang with the homies
But they got me if they need me, den it's on G*

Everybody calls me "young buck" when they see me. The cops ride by all slow. Grit on everybody. We grit right back. Sometimes they jump out and search everybody.

"What's wrong?" they ask as soon as they see my long face. I tell 10 Gs the deal.

"A white bitch?" Ted blurts out like he's asking the whole city. "She's white?" I just nod—*yeah, man*. "Come on, man, don't tell me that. Tell me something else, anything. Tell me

* "Out on Bail," 2pac, 1994.

he shot somebody, tell me he robbed a bank, tell me whatever. Just don't tell me this—white!"

"In Arizona too? Damn Oohwop," D-Rock says. D-Rock looks like he lives on a bench in Fisher Park. He's wearing what he always wears: greasy army fatigues and a military hat on some Black Moon shit. He calls it BDU—basic dress uniform. Cargos. Camos. Velcro. Gore-Tex. Kevlar. That's his bag. "'Cause I'm a mothafuckin soldier," he told me one day when I asked why he wears the same shit every day.

D-Rock calls himself the hood scientist. He hates the white man but loves white pussy. He's always got a white jawn with him.

"Fuckin Arizona!" Ted shakes his head. "Of all places!"

Population none in the desert and sun
With a gun cracker running things under his thumb*

"It's racist as shit out there, man," Scoop says.

"I know," Ted says, "they don't even take off for Dr. King's birthday."

"Vicious. What?"

"Yeah man, you ain't know that?"

"Crazy."

"It ain't like you gotta recite 'I Have a Dream' or some shit."

"It's just a day off work," Ted says. "But they'd rather go to work than take a day off for a black man."

"They straight-up hate us out there. Fuckin hot-ass desert," D-Rock says.

* "By the Time I Get to Arizona," Public Enemy, 1991.

"And a straight-up Philly ngh like Uzi?" Scoop says. "They don't want him comin home till Neveruary!"

"The judge might try to roof him. The white man don't like you messing with his little Suzie."

"They can't give him no wheel of death for that."

"What's the wheel of death?"

"Life."

This all feels like broken glass in my mind.

"Did you talk to him?" Ted asks. "What did he say?"

I hear Uzi: *Get me outta here!*

Dear Carole,

Malo ran away. Not like the time he ran away when he was five years old, when he just went to the end of the block and looked to see if I was looking. No, this time he really ran away. He's fourteen.

The thing is—he took my car. What kind of running away is that? Not only is my child gone, but my ride too. Initially I think he'll return in the evening. I'm upset but not worried. But when nighttime comes and he doesn't return, I get worried. I think about calling the police. Chaka says that we should wait. I call everyone I know but no one has seen or heard from Malo and I don't know his friends' phone numbers.

Morning comes and Malo still hasn't come home. I decide to call the police. The police seem uninterested in finding a runaway black boy but they take down the information. I don't want to report the car stolen because that will criminalize Malo.

Malo ran away but there wasn't an argument and he

wasn't on punishment, so I'm baffled. Where is he and why did he leave? Of course this means he isn't going to school, but I'm not even thinking about school, I just want to make sure that he is safe. Chaka doesn't seem worried but I'm sure he is. We are both amazed that he took my car but I had information that Chaka didn't. I know that Malo had taken my car many times while I was asleep and his father was away. So while it was definitely outrageous that Malo took my car, since he's only fourteen and doesn't have a license or even a permit, I wasn't that shocked.

Then after a week, he strolls in. I ask Malo, what was he thinking? He simply says that he was ready to live on his own. If I wasn't so angry, I would have laughed. Actually, I did laugh. What chutzpah! Where did he get the nerve? Well, I really don't have to look too far.

I ran away when I was thirteen too. I not only ran away but I left a note for my mother saying that I was running away to get married and that she shouldn't look for me. I left in the middle of the night and took the subway to the 34th Street bus terminal and took a bus to Reading, PA! I arrived in Reading with nothing but the clothes on my back and called my aunt Patrice from the bus station and asked her to come get me.

There was an incident that made me run away. My mother wouldn't let me go to a beach party that a lot of my friends were going to and I was very angry about it. My mother and I didn't have a good relationship and I wanted to get away. My aunt Jaime had taken me to Reading when I was six years old and I had fond memories of Reading. For one thing, my aunt Patrice had a house and that seemed like the ultimate luxury to me. Little did I know at the time that Heller's Court was called "Hell's Court" for a reason.

I took money out of my aunt Jaime's purse. I am sure that my mother caught grief about that but I wasn't thinking about that at the time. My mother finally called my aunt Patrice and my aunt admitted that I was there. My mother didn't come get me. I don't even think that she talked to me. She was angry with my aunt Patrice for not calling her but at least she knew where I was.

Reading was wild, and even though I wanted more freedom, this was a life that was full of chaos and violence. My cousin Junie was the only child and he was wild. I saw him pick up a butcher knife and chase his mother with it. He was my age and he already had a baby. My uncle Franky and aunt Patrice ran a speakeasy on the weekend so there were lots of people coming in and out from Friday night to Sunday. They sold liquor, drank, argued, and fought a lot. This was all new to me, as my mother didn't drink. The only fights that I saw in my home were my aunt Jaime and my mother arguing. The worst that they said to each other was to call each other a bitch. My aunt called my mother a "yellow bitch" and my mom retaliated by called my aunt a "black bitch."

But this was on a different level. Knives and alcohol and cussing were an everyday thing, and on the weekend, it was all day. I enrolled in school and that was a culture shock. It was mainly white. My high school in Brooklyn was mixed but this school was basically white. But I think that I could have handled the school if the home situation wasn't so volatile.

Two things happened that brought my stay in Reading to an end. My aunt took me with her one afternoon to a "friend's" house. She told me to stay in an outer room while she went into a bedroom with a young man. I was her alibi. She would tell my uncle Franky that she was with me, and that would be the end of that. I had seen a lot but this was something that she chose to do. Then my aunt accused me of trying to be with Uncle Franky. Reading, PA, made cream sodas that were red, and this absolutely delighted me as I loved cream soda and the idea of red cream soda was wonderful. Uncle Franky would bring me cream soda when he came home from work and I loved it. My aunt took this as a flirtation with my uncle Franky. There was no such thing going on in my mind. And mind you, this was the woman who took me to a house where she had a rendezvous with a lover.

So after three months in Reading, I called my mother and asked to come home. I don't think that my mother said a word to me all the way home.

Malo and I don't speak either.

God, give me strength.

Amina

10

Bail Money

"It's just like my daddy told me," my dad says. "I ain't got no bail money. Not a dime!" He swipes his keys. "None." I haven't seen my dad since my mom got back from the psych ward. He's home now, just for a hot minute, before he goes out of town again.

"If we don't help him, the system will hang him," Mom says. "You know that's what they do to black boys. You know that, Chaka!"

"That boy hung himself a long time ago! Why are you so surprised? He's never done the right thing. Never!"

"He made a mistake. Wrong place, wrong time. He's our son—we will profit by or pay for whatever he becomes."

"He raped a girl."

"Don't say that," my mom erupts, wincing at the very thought.

"A white girl! My enemies will love this."

"Statutory rape!"

"A white girl!"

"It was consensual. He's only seventeen, she told him she was sixteen."

"Well, she was thirteen!"

"He didn't know. My son is not a rapist!"

"He's a thug. You reap what you sow," he says like a southern preacher.

"Please," she pleads. "They'll do him like Emmett Till if we don't."

Something in the kitchen falls. I feel like everything is falling, crashing around me.

"He's not working. He's not in school. Can't you see? He's destroying you."

"You don't understand."

"What don't I understand?"

"What it's like . . . for a mother."

Later on I get on the computer, a Mac Performa 5200. I dial up the Internet and type in "Emmett Till" on this new thing my dad's friend Zizwe told me about called Google. It's dope, you can find anything on this jawn . . . including all the hardcore Afro-Centrix flicks. I read about how in 1955, Emmett, fourteen years old like me, got killed for whistling at a white woman in Philadelphia, Mississippi. But they didn't just kill him. They shot his ears off at point-blank range. Gouged his eyes out. Tied him with barbed wire by his neck. Cut his dick off. Dumped him in the Tallahatchie River. There's two pictures of him. One where he's alive, glowing, wearing a fedora and a boyish grin, looking like Uzi, actually. And another, in his casket, his face deformed like melted plastic. My soul cries for Till like he was Uzi.

I say to my dad, "So you really not going to help my brother?"

"I can't help him. He made his bed, now he has to lie in it. One day you'll make yours too, and you'll have to lie in it."

Dear Carole,

If I could run, hide from bad news, I would be on the other side of the world. Bad news has ridden the hem of my skirts and I haven't been able to dance the news away. Now bad news has arrived big-time and in this midnight hour, when everyone is asleep and only the TV talks, I am speechless but full of fear. Fear for my child. The one that I put on the plane to Arizona. The child that I wanted to save and didn't know what to do. My firstborn child, who was full of life and too much mischief. He is in jail facing what?

God, give me strength.

Amina

11

Xmas in AZ

Xmas in AZ. Nobody's in this Holiday Inn except me and my mom. We're here to see Uzi. My mom still hasn't spoken to him and no one knows what's going on.

We're supposed to see this lawyer she got for Uzi, Mr. Dodds or something.

"I had to borrow money to get this attorney," she tells me. "A lot of money. Your father doesn't know."

She doesn't have to tell me not to say anything. It's understood.

"I don't have the money for this," she keeps repeating over and over. "I can't continue to rob Peter to pay Paul."

At first she tried to front like she didn't want me to come to Arizona. "You have school."

"Fuck school," I blurted out before I could catch myself.

"Khumalo!"

"I'm saying, though, this is more important than school.

God first, family next, everyone else take a number and get in line, right?"

"Right."

"Plus I don't want you going out there solo-dolo," I said.

I already knew my dad wasn't coming. She didn't have to tell me. It was understood.

When 10 Gs found out I was going to Arizona, they got mad hype.

"Gotta give him the hood news: Tone got killed down Badlands. Shelly's pregnant. Kierra just had her second baby. Kirk got locked up. Cool C and Steady B tried to rob the PNC and killed this black lady cop. They gave Steady B life and C is on death row. Gas is up, coke is down, crack is always up, syrup and zannies are up, weed is down . . . It ain't good news, it's hood news!"

"Anything else?"

"Tell him to keep his head up."

One time I told Uzi I'd go anywhere or anyplace for him. On the way to the hotel, driving through the desert with my mom—passing signs for Indian casinos and wild horses—I'm thinking this is it: anywhere, anyplace. The air conditioner in the rental car is weak and it feels like we're swimming through the ninety-degree heat. The tips of our noses are beaded with sweat.

—

"Merry Christmas," the lady at the front desk says.

"Merry Christmas," my mom says just to be nice. We don't really celebrate Christmas at home.

"We can't celebrate some big fat white man bringing us gifts" is what my dad said when I asked him about it a few years ago. "When? Tell me when has the white man ever brought us gifts?" Guess he's got a point.

Even though we don't celebrate it, I know what Christmas feels like, what it sounds like, what it looks like—and this ain't it. Everything about this picture is off: the hot weather, the cactus in the lobby with sloppy Christmas lights slung over it, Uzi in jail.

"So what brings you to Arizona?" she asks as she checks us in.

My mom's face says, *Mind yours.*

We don't even know what jail Uzi's in or anything.

The lawyer is an old white dude with a comb-over. Every time he talks, his hair moves like a furry mouthpiece. Greasy gold watch strapped to his hairy wrist. His shoes are Armor All shiny.

"I was a cop for twenty-five years," he says, "so I understand both sides. I've—"

"So whose side are you on?" I say.

"I've been a defense attorney for the last twenty years."

"But whose side are you on? My math says we're down by five years."

I can tell we're just another number to him. I see it in the blankness in his eyes, the distance in his glare.

"I'm going to work to reduce his sentence as much as possible."

Just another pitiful family, that's probably what he thinks. He doesn't know how strong we are, though. Doesn't know where we come from. Doesn't know that it wasn't always like this. I think about how it was when I was young. How my dad would take me and Uzi to the park in front of the Rocky statue. How we'd play football for hours and yell "Cunningham" before each throw. How we'd run up the Art Museum steps before we left. How happy we were.

"They're going to try to try him as an adult since he'll be eighteen by the trial date. I'm going to push for getting him tried as a juvenile since he was seventeen when the incident occurred." He goes on and on and on with the bad weather: *clouds, rain, storms*—

"Just stop. I need to see my son."

> **Saw the light, caught a case, couldn't afford to fight**
> **Lawyer white, had to cop out or face more than life***

"As you know, he's in solitary," he says. "Twenty-three-hour lockdown. He's got one free hour each day. That's your hour. You'll be behind glass."

My eyes tear with pain and rage thinking about Uzi in that black hole all day, wasting away. It's torture. They're torturing my brother, torturing my mom, torturing me. I want to break down and weep but I gotta be strong for Moms.

* "Trading Places," AZ, 1997.

—

Everything inside the jail—benches, tables, lockers, rails—is metal and shiny. A sparkling hell. All the visitors are women except for me, and they're mostly black and Mexicans. Mothers, daughters, wives, girlfriends, side chicks. No fathers, though. Not mine, not Uzi's, not nobody's.

All the guards are white as bone. Stiff muhfuckas with buzz cuts, sharp square jaws, and Oakley shades.

Uzi on the other side of the glass like Koreans at the corner store back in Philly.

"I didn't do nothing," he tells us.

"Well, you did something," my mom says. "Or else why are we here?"

"I mean, I fucked her, but Ma, she said she was sixteen."

"And you believed her?"

"You would too if you saw her, she's like a thirty-six triple D," showing us with his hands. We laugh a little, just to keep from crying. I see his beard coming in, thick and black like the Sunnis in Philly.

"Get me outta here," he says, like we have the key somewhere, like we ain't lost in the system too.

My mom's face is steely. She's wearing her mask, trying to hide her emotions, but I'm close enough to smell her pain. She never wears her heart on her face in public.

"We're working on it," she says.

"They got me in a dog kennel, yo. Like I'm a Rottweiler! All I can do is squat and run in place! Just please get me outta here."

"It's not that easy."

"But I didn't do anything!"

"Yes you did. You're going to have to get over that. The law is the law."

"Can't you use your clout?"

"Clout?" She laughs.

"Can't you and Dad use your clout?"

"Clout, Daudi? What does that mean? Clout didn't stop them from arresting you. Clout didn't stop them from putting you in the hole. Clout didn't make your case a case of youthful indiscretion." She shakes her head, lost. "They don't look at me and see an educator, a choreographer that's traveled the world. They see a nigger. A nigger." The guard is coming for Uzi.

"We have no clout . . . just each other," she says.

Time's up.

Uzi puts his fist on the glass. I do too.

"One love." I swear I can feel his knuckles through the glass.

"One."

In the car on our way back to the hotel, the radio plays holiday hits. My mom hums along to "Whose Child Is This?" The speakers tremble.

"I wish he was in a Philly jail," I say to my mom.

"Whether he's here or in Philly," she says, "jail is jail. Chains are chains."

Some fortunate, some less fortunate

Some get it, some get acquitted*

* "Unfortunate," RAM Squad, 1996.

Uzi's day in court.

"The plan is for him to come back to Philadelphia with us," my mom tells me on our way into the courtroom. "Dodds said the court can transfer his probation to Philly. That's what I spent all that money I didn't have for—to bring Daudi home. I want you to pray on it."

"Okay, I will." I don't pray a lot, but I'm down to try anything. I close my eyes and see the face of Emmett Till.

I try not to think about Till now as I sit in the courtroom. The cold benches remind me of the Meeting for Worship benches at Foes. Mom's got her hair pulled back tight. I can see all the tiny veins swimming across her temple.

They bring my brother out in handcuffs and shackles like O.J. His light blue button-up tucked into khakis. He looks like he's on a job interview. He sees me, nods. I give him a strong nod that says, *Everything's going to be all right*. Then a smile that says, *You're still my hero, everybody makes mistakes*.

The judge has a face that looks like old, low-hanging fruit. His voice sounds distant, like he's a hundred miles away.

My dad's friend Bobby Seale is one of the founders of the Black Panthers. One day in the hallway at Temple University Bobby told me about how the Panthers, strapped with Kalashnikovs and rocking cold black shades, cocked berets, and leather trenches, used to take over courtrooms. He told me that the only justice you get is the justice you take.

"So the concept is this, basically," Bobby once said in a speech. "The whole black nation has to be put together as a black army. And we gon' walk on this nation, we gon' walk on this racist power structure, and we gon' say to the whole damn government: Stick 'em up, motherfucker! This is a holdup! We come for what's ours!"

I wish I was a Black Panther right now.

We come for what's ours . . . and his name is Uzi, I'd say.

I strike America like a case of heart disease
Panther power is running through my arteries*

"Will the defendant approach . . ."

I pray the only prayer I know, one my parents taught me when I was little: *We call upon the Most High and the ancestors, far and near . . .*

"Young man . . ."

Mothers of our mothers, fathers of our fathers . . .

"Menace to society . . . burden to this community . . ."

To render us mercy and to bear witness . . .

"By the power . . . Arizona . . ."

For the liberation and victory of all oppressed people.

"Hereby . . . guilty! . . . Ten years . . ."

Amen.

I carry my mom out of the courtroom, onto the plane, and back to Philly. We don't talk, we can't speak.

Dear Carole,

Chaka is always saying he needs space. I know what that means. He needs space away from me. And the more space the better.

Space so as not to be reminded that I am broken,

* "Panther Power," 2Pac, 1991.

space so as not to be reminded Daudi is broken. Malo is breaking.

I'm broken. "Fix Me, Jesus" is the spiritual that I loved so much when I was a little girl in Brooklyn. "Fix me, Jesus, Fix me." That's what sanatoriums were for. Places that "fixed" people with problems. Twice I've been committed and twice I've returned home feeling the same and seeing the same. The visits were remarkable in their inability to even scratch the surface of what's wrong, if anything was wrong. If you say something is wrong enough times, everyone begins to believe it, including me. Okay, fix me, damn it! How can you fix someone who isn't broken? I'm aching, I'm in pain, but broken—no!

No one knew that I was in the sanatorium, just Chaka and Malo. My mom didn't know. What happens when a person disappears for two months? What do you say? I didn't know because I wasn't the one doing the telling. I was being fixed! One of the patients at the hospital asked for something and was denied. She said, "For nine hundred dollars a day, I should be getting more than Jell-O and a blanket." It was funny to me at the time because I agreed. It was also funny because the young woman was so rational in such an irrational place. I had enjoyed taking walks around the grounds. I could think. I could control those walks. I was safe. Safe but not fixed.

Years ago, I straddled Chaka, beating him in the face, telling him how much he had broken my heart. His response was "That's it, I am gone." He didn't leave that night, but it is just a matter of time. What do I do with "You are sewn into my gut" and "You are the smartest woman I have ever met"? I treasure his words as always. He had come home late that night, very late, and it was too much. How much more could I take? I didn't know what to say to him but I wished I had said, "Remember, just remember!"

God, give me strength.

Amina

12

The Line

"Winning is the deodorant that covers all stink," Coach says. Tells me as long as we keep winning, he'll keep Roach away from me. That's our deal.

It's the fourth quarter and we're down by three—54 to 57—to our rivals, Hilltop. Big game. Like twenty seconds left. I'm dribbling at the top of the key.

Championship banners hang above my head like quilts on a clothesline. Bleachers full of parents and friends. Nia's here with one of her girlfriends. Amir's standing with Ryan near the exit.

Basketball clears my mind, takes me away from the bullshit. On the court, I'm the judge.

I play my heart out.

My Jordans squeaking across the blond wood. It's like a high-pitched language—call and response—I speak with my sneaks. They're repeating the lines from a Jordan movie that Uzi got for me a few birthdays ago.

"Once I get the ball, you're at my mercy. There's nothing you can say or do about it. I own the ball. I own the game. I own the guy guarding me. I can actually play him like a puppet." I love Jordan's heart, his determination. I remember Game 5 of the NBA Finals against the Utah Jazz, he had the flu and he played anyway. During every time-out, every dead ball, you could see the sickness in his eyes. The end of the game, tie game, he hit a three to win it. They had to carry him off the gym floor, he was so weak.

Later, they asked him about it: "I didn't want to give up. No matter how sick I was, no matter how tired I was, no matter how low on energy I was. I felt an obligation to my teammates and the city of Chicago to go out and give that extra effort."

I'm dribbling, crossing over, spinning, faking, pumping, passing . . . I get the ball back—dribble, spin, hesitate, reverse, penetrate . . . driving hard to the paint.

Foul.

I'm at the line. Season on the line. Everything on the line.

Coach calls a time-out.

"I need you to come through," he says, both hands on my shoulders. "It's on you. I know you can handle it."

I step to the line, my toes kissing the stripe. The ref, whistle hanging out of his mouth like a Marlboro, bounces the rock to me. I spin the ball in my hand. Bounce, spin, bounce-

bounce, spin. Spread my fingers across it like a phat ass. Let my fingertips find the crack, settle in.

The ball leaves my hand
    It's up in the air . . .

Dear Carole,

I spent the night in my car. It was funny sleeping in Fisher Park. I come home in the morning and see Chaka as he's leaving for work. He doesn't speak and neither do I. I think he is ashamed of me. It is hard for me to acknowledge this but it is true. He doesn't want to be seen with me. He doesn't say anything but his actions tell me that.

True, I am terribly overweight and I am not the small dancer that he met a long time ago. It is a hell that I seem to have imposed on myself. Why? There are probably many reasons. I resent him for being ashamed and I draw farther away from him. Every houseguest and visitor is my responsibility but our world is a secret. The façade of a marriage and a happy home is just that. Perhaps the houseguests are distractions and keep the attention away from us. I only know that the silence has me basking in invisible rhythms and I have disappeared.

My weight is another mask for the pain. Am I conscious of it? Yes and no. I run away from my image but it follows me, and even when I am not looking, others are looking and sometimes those looks usher in comments. "I didn't recognize you; how did you gain so much weight?" "Why did you gain so much weight?" "How in the world does a dancer gain so much weight?" They were questions I had asked myself a thousand times. "Pain" is all I can say. Chaka hates it, I hate it, but we all dance around it.

God, give me strength.

Amina

13

Midnight Train

The coldest day of the year. That disrespectful *brrr*. Outside it looks like everybody's blazing big blunts. Swirling dark clouds roll in like waves.

I'm in the living room watching Kung Fu Theater on Channel 48. I hear my mom and dad in the kitchen, their voices rising, falling, crashing like distant thunder.

Maybe all this arguing is good, I think. Maybe it means they still care. Like, it shows they're still willing to fight for each other. Maybe not fighting is worse.

This flick is called *Shogun Assassin*. Samurais in straw hats sword-fighting in the desert. A little boy flashes on the screen:

> When I was little my father was famous. He was the greatest samurai in the empire and he was the shogun's decapitator. He cut off the heads of 131 lords. It was a bad time for the empire. The shogun just stayed inside his castle and he never came out. People said his brain

was infected by devils. My father would come home; he would forget about the killings. He wasn't scared of the shogun, but the shogun was of him. Maybe that was the problem. Then one night the shogun sent his ninja spies to our house. They were supposed to kill my father but they didn't. That was the night everything changed.

I hear fists slamming on the counter—my cue to see what's going on.

"He's leaving," my mom screams as I walk in the kitchen. *Leaving to go where?* I think.

I see my dad. His face looks cold and tight. He's wearing a black dashiki with an ankh on it. The ankh symbolizes life in Egyptian mythology. Death in Philly reality.

I remember something my dad said when my grandfather died: "He thought of leaving for good every time he heard the long, mournful whistle of the train." He told me it's called "wanderlust"—that need to go, to bounce—and that all the men in my family have it.

My mom hangs on him like a peacoat. He drags her, slow and determined like a wounded soldier. Mom's tears flowing like the Schuylkill River. I've never seen them like this.

"Hold up." I hold my hand out like a crossing guard. "Where you going?"

"We'll talk about it later," he says.

Later? Who does he take me for, hitting me with later, like I'm some little kid? I know later never comes.

"Nah, we gon' talk about it now!" I get loud. His mind is made up, though.

He's rushing to the door, whooshing like wind through vents, gripping a beat-up black leather bag. That bag's been everywhere; it spends more time with Pops than I do.

"How can you? How can you? Leave us . . . like this?" my mom sobs, looking right at me, her heavy eyes begging me to do something. The movement is moving and there's nothing I can do. *Fuck am I gonna do?* I jump in front of him, try to block him, but he just steps around me.

"I have to go," is what he says. "I just have to go."

"Go where?"

"Just. Go," he says opening the door. "One day you'll understand."

"Fuck one day! Fuck tomorrow!"

Our eyes lock. Tears glisten in his. Rage in mine.

"See?" He looks at my mom, shaking his head. "He has no respect for his father."

"It's my fault? He doesn't respect you because you're never here."

He's at the door now, palming the knob.

I say, "I'll respect you even less if you walk out that door," but it's too late. The door flies open, a cold rush, he's gone.

I feel my veins turn icy and my soul drift into darkness as he turns his back on us and marches into winter.

Mom falls into me, her wet face against my Hilfiger hoodie. The screen door stutters shut. I lift my mom up under the arms. She's deadweight. I hold her tight and feel her back expanding in my palms like dough. I didn't know she was *this* heavy. You never know how heavy anyone is until you have to carry them.

I wonder if he's leaving because of her weight.

The other day, looking through her journal, I found this old school photo of her from back in the day. She was a dime. Dancer body, silky skin, the glow of a movie star, Lena Horne or somebody like that. Classic beauty. She's a dancer that doesn't dance anymore, not even her eyes. There's no music, just pain. It's hard to imagine that the lady in that faded photo is the same woman I'm holding now. She's all I have.

"Protect me, Malo," she says through a mouthful of tears.

From what? I think. *Everything, I guess.*

"I will." Putting my hand on her shoulder, rubbing the fist-size knots on her back. She's as fragile as her thin eyelashes.

All night she sobs. I try to comfort her, sitting on her bed, massaging her head. She's just sobbing. She can't even look at me. Her eyes are shut with tears. The cries last forever. The whole neighborhood can probably hear her wailing. When I leave the crib, she's sobbing. When I get back, it's like I never left.

"You need anything, Ma?"

"To die."

14

North of Death

I'm choking this bottle of Henny, taking swigs with Amir and Scoop. The brown burns my whole face up.

"Hennessy make plenty enemies," Scoop rumbles, slugging the gnac down like it's water. Sometimes, like now, Scoop reminds me of Uzi, with his wild energy and crazy stories and temper as sudden as gunshots.

She said, Afrocentricity was of the past
so she got into R&B, hip-house, bass, and jazz*

We're in the jaws of the night, in front of this row house on a back block in North Philly near Diamond Street.

"North side of death," Amir says.

Scoop shows us his new gun, a black Desert Eagle. It's midnight black, fat, and long. "His name is Mr. Nipples," Scoop

* "I Used to Love H.E.R. (Hearing Every Rhyme)," Common, 1994.

says, Cookie Monster eyes wobbling. "Turning legs into wheels." It's huge, with a scope on it like something off *Terminator*.

"Damn, Scoop," I say, a little scared.

"What? You thought I was playing? You think it's a game?" We hear police sirens searching in the distance.

"Just don't get caught with that," Amir says.

"Rather be caught with it than without it. Rather go to jail than die young."

A door the color of Pepto-Bismol, manned by some dude in black shades with a Sunni beard. Scoop daps him and we're in.

Boom boom boom—the bass from Luke's "Face Down Ass Up" is beating up the house, pounding, thumping. *Face down ass up / That's the way we like to fuck . . .*

The steps are dark, steep, and sticky with drink. Scoop's in front walking his superthug walk, fist clenched, marching on some one-two, one-two shit. *Pussy ain't nuttin but meat on the bone / Suck it or fuck it or leave it alone . . .*

Upstairs is crazier than a Luke video.

Girls, naked or in neon G-strings, dancing everywhere. A blur of clapping asses. A buffet of shapes: teardrops, bubbles, apples, cherries, pears, hearts, and straight-up ghetto booties. Instant wood in my Guess jeans.

Smoke swirls through the darkness, curling slow like storm clouds.

We take another shot of Henny.

A bunch of shady nghz in the shadows. Everybody's way older than us. Me and Amir are fourteen.

The stage is porn.

"Pussy Olympics," Scoop says.

One girl, legs behind her neck like a pretzel, has three lit candles hanging from her pussy, pushing them in and out like a flamethrower. Two other chicks bumping butts with a purple dildo inside them both. Another jawn upside down on a pole.

There's a guy with a mic—the host, I guess—giving a play-by-play and encouraging the girls. "This is where the ballers come to play and where the players come to ball." He's smoking a Black & Mild. He blows the pussy candles out—"Lights out"—then puts the mouthpiece of his cigar in her pussy. "Smoke that," he laughs, making faces as the cigar tip glows orange and her pussy puffs.

Shot.

I feel the Henny all through my body like a 12-gauge shotty.

I'm standing next to a couple of thumping Kenwoods, footprint against the wall. The bass owns me.

My eyes lock on this short, bowlegged girl. She shuffles over and poses for me, bending over and touching the floor with her hands. Her thighs, shiny with baby oil, look like glazed hams.

"You dancin or datin?" she asks.

"Huh?"

"Dancin or datin?" she says, rubbing her pussy.

"Datin? You wanna go on a date?" I'm confused.

"Datin means fuckin," Scoop laughs.

"How much?"

"A buck," she says, dropping to the floor. She spreads her legs like a peace sign and flicks her pierced tongue at me.

"A hunnit?"

"Yeah."

"I'm cool."

Amir jumps in. "We get it for free."

"Nothing's free," Scoop says. "With hoes, somehow you always pay. Always."

Three folding chairs crash onto the stage.

"Are y'all ready for tonight's main event?" the host asks.

I'm looking around at the freak show going on everywhere, wondering, *How is this not the main event?* The crowd howls, hoots, and grunts as three strippers climb onstage.

"Y'all not ready for this," he says, setting the chairs up. "But we gon' give it to you anyway. Listen, I need three volunteers, three volunteers."

Amir bolts toward the stage like it's the halftime shot for a million dollars at the Sixers game. Two more thirsty dudes follow.

"Let's get this dick-sucking contest started!"

Me and Amir lock eyes, like *What the fuck?* His smile is bright against his black face. Scoop is laughing, nodding, and pulling out wads of cash from different pockets.

"Fellas, take a seat. Ladies, introduce yourselves."

"Buffy."

"Honey."

"Diamond."

"Ain't none of them dimes," Scoop says. "More like fives and sixes with scars and stitches." Diamond is the one on Amir. She's old, at least triple his age, with tits that hang like wet socks.

"Make ya bets right here." The host is taking money.

"A dub on Honey . . . a buck on Buffy . . . fifty on Diamond," different people yell.

Scoop makes his bet and throws a knot down.

It's like the hood version of the stock market. I see the money flapping, the asses clapping, and think about the power of the dollar.

"Hoes, on your marks." Pulls off his watch to keep time. They hit their knees.

"Set." They whip out condoms and roll them on.

"Go!"

Everyone in the room is going crazy, screaming and shouting.

"Lawd have mercy, she suckin the earth, wind, and fire out his dick!"

"She suckin the black off his shit!"

It's over faster than a Tyson fight. Amir's girl pulls up and snaps her fingers fast in the air.

"We got a winner," the host announces. "Diamond!" She holds the condom up like a freshly caught fish.

"Official time: one minute, twenty-one seconds."

Dear Carole,

Kianna is still in love with Scoop. He lives around the corner with his sister, Alicia. I don't know what he does but he lives a thug lifestyle. Kianna is the first one besides me to go to college but it is clear to me that Scoop is everything to her. A first love is difficult, particularly for a girl.

Scoop is part of the crew. Ted, Damien (D-Rock), Daudi, and now Malo. Malo and Scoop have became close since Daudi left. Too close! It is a strange connection, as Scoop is around Daudi's age, but perhaps Scoop fills a void for Malo. Malo has always been one to hang with the older crowd with the exception of his best friend, Amir. I know that they all smoke weed but I don't know what else they do. Malo smokes too and that was another thing that I warned him about, but he didn't listen. I know that they are all sexually active including Malo. He doesn't have to tell me. The evidence is all over the place. None of them work and their idea of being busy is getting high. Malo doesn't really talk to me. I wish I knew what was on his mind. The only thing that's clear to me is his pain.

I know Scoop's and Ted's parents through them. I ask about them and they tell me tidbits that give me an idea of their family life. I know Ted's parents are very socially active. They want to move to a bigger house in Blue Bell. The only thing that I know about Blue Bell is that Patti LaBelle once belonged to a trio called the Blue Bells. When she was asked about the name, she said that she got the name from a very upscale suburb of Philadelphia, someplace that she aspired to live. I know that Scoop's father is somewhat older than his mom. Ted's mom and dad went to Lincoln University and were college sweethearts. Scoop's sister, Alicia, has a young son who is very smart and precocious and apparently his father is a

Jamaican drug dealer. I learn all of this knowledge through Malo but it is usually true.

Malo has the best chance to make it, not because he is exempt from mischief and even mayhem but because he is a listener and observer. Like his brother, though, he is choosing a thug life. My only hope is that he is mortified by the consequences of that life.

God, give me strength.

Amina

15

Broke

I go to steal my mom's car and there's already someone stealing it. I've been doing this since I was fourteen, taking my mom's wheel in the middle of the night, driving around the city with Amir.

"You about to get fucked up," I yell at the thief.

Next I'm staring down the barrel of his gun, a chrome tunnel to the other side, as he steals the car.

"He didn't steal it," my mom whispers. She winces while she talks, like every word hurts to say. "The bank owns it."

"He stole it," I say. "And all my CDs in the backseat too."

"We're bankrupt."

"How?"

"If you don't understand money, it grows wings and poof—it's gone."

"What does that even mean . . . being bankrupt?"

She's sitting in the La-Z-Boy she never gets up from. Her sadness bolts her to the chair like the Death Row Records logo. She's paralyzed like how my grandfather was. She's faded too, high as a kite, eyes glazed like shiny marbles. White paste in the creases of her mouth like she's been talking way too long. She doesn't say much, though. Pill bottles, Diet Coke, empty Häagen-Dazs containers, and bills form rings around her like Saturn. TV on—*Cops* as usual. Every night, *Bad boys, bad boys, whatcha gonna do, whatcha gonna do when they come for you*. That shit creeps me out. Makes me think about Uzi. Maybe it makes her think about Uzi too? Maybe that's why she watches? I see Uzi in her shattered face.

Her purse is like CVS, a blur of brown plastic bottles with *X*'s and *Z*'s. She's got a fistful of pills, all fruity colors like Wild Berry Skittles.

Yo, this ngh named D-rugs, my moms dates him
Swear to God I hate him, if I could I would break him*

"It means we're broke, Daudi." She pops the orange pill.

"I'm not Daahoud, Mom." She doesn't respond, just looks me over all floaty-eyed.

"What about Dad?"

"He's bankrupt too . . . and in trouble with the IRS." Red.

How can people who've been working their whole lives be broke? How can people who've been struggling their whole lives still be struggling? Is this what my dad means when he says the struggle continues? But when does it end? Something's off about this picture. Fuck this broke-ass picture.

* "D Rugs," Cam'ron, 1998.

"I know, Daudi," she says, like I'm my brother. She keeps calling me that lately. "When it rains it pours." Purple. She's crying without tears. "When you grow up hungry," she says, "you promise yourself you'll never be hungry again."

"I promise to get us out of this," I say.

"I know, Daudi."

"It's me, Ma, Malo," I try to correct her. But she's fading out now like the dope fiends who wash cars on Broad and Godfrey. "I'ma get us out of this, Mom."

"I know, Daudi."

Dear Carole,

I've never seen Malo so angry. He's slamming things. His cheeks are puffy. I ask his coach if something happened. He says that "they lost" but that "Malo played well."

I ask Malo, "What happened?" He doesn't say anything but I can feel him respond.

"I know that you lost the game but I heard you played well." I feel his body hiccup, as if to say, How could I play well if my team lost? I continued, "Sometimes we lose, but if we try our best, that is all we can do." That got a rise out of him. He turned over and looked at me and said in a stern voice, "We lost!"

I know what he means: I lost, Mom, and I don't ever want to lose again! I wasn't going to get much further with "as long as you give it your best."

Losing isn't an option for Malo and it hurt. I understand that for Malo, losing was akin to something that I have never experienced. He was upset at himself because he felt that he could have saved the game and he didn't. He was upset that an event that involved him had not gone well. Never mind his teammates; he had lost and right now that was all that mattered.

Losing isn't the flip side of winning for Malo. It is all or it simply isn't. From the very beginning of his life, it was win by any means necessary. If I tapped him lightly, he responded more forcibly just to make sure if it were combat, I would know that he was ready. Where does he get that? If he fought with Daudi and he was losing, he would change the rules so that Daudi was punished. I'm the unwitting foil in the Malo book of rules. Win at any cost. He will go for the jugular and not think anything about it. When I finally wise up to his tricks, he is not repentant and is already on to bigger and better things. Malo has always been fearless. I pray that this quality doesn't get him into trouble later on in his life.

God, give me strength.

Amina

16

A Hunnit Knuckles

Ted hollers, “These are the Thug Life codes all UPK members shall live and die by.” We’re huddled in the parking lot behind Cardinal Dougherty High School, under a big gray sky smoky with overcast.

The whole crew—like a hunnit knuckles—rushes me and Amir like a sandstorm.

“One: You got three options: (a) get rich, (b) get sent to jail, or (c) get killed.”

I catch a punch to the back of my head. “UPK!” they keep shouting. I squint up at the silver overcast sky, then trip into Amir—we swing on everything moving.

“Two: Your word is your bond.”

A dozen flying fists landing everywhere like hail.

“Three: One crew’s rat is every crew’s rat. Snitches get stitches. We don’t talk to police. No fish ever got caught with its mouth shut.”

I bust a lip—then get mine bust . . . head shots like tambourines on Sundays.

Gotta put you on your ass to see what it does to you
When you stand up and see that I'm just showin love to you*

"Four: Money over bitches. Chasing bitches, you'll run out of money. But chasing money, you'll never run out of bitches."

Stumbling backward . . . me and Amir, back to back, sucking air before we go buck . . .

"Five: No slinging in schools . . . Slinging to little children or having little children slinging is against the Code."

Hooks and haymakers.

"Six: In unity, there is strength!"

Uppercuts, crosses, and chaos.

"Seven: The boys in blue don't run nothing—we do! We control the hood and make it safe for squares."

Blood flies from my nose.

"Eight: No slinging to pregnant sisters. That's baby killing and therefore genocide!"

I'm falling into different-colored rooms—orange/red/purple/black.

"Nine: Know your target, who's the real enemy . . . Civilians are not a target and should be spared in hood warfare."

A body shot takes me to my knees. "UPK!" Amir's blood in my eye.

* "Bring It On," DMX, 1998.

"Ten: Harm to babies and old people will not be forgiven."

Timb boots stomping me like a welcome mat.

"Eleven: No rape."

I ball up, knees to forehead . . . and then I don't feel any pain anymore.

"Twelve: Respect brothers and sisters if they respect themselves."

I tackle a body, land on my feet, and swing for the hills.

"Thirteen: No shooting at parties."

Nothing but air . . . everyone moves away . . . I cough up gravel and blood. A great big bear hug.

"Fourteen: Know the Code. Be a real ngh. Be down with the Code of Thug Life."

I fight out of the hug . . . keep swinging . . . punching, kicking, grabbing, tackling . . . they're trying to get me to stop but I won't, fuck that, I'm out for blood . . . I swing . . . swing . . . keep fighting and fuckin fighting until they're all piled on top of me and I can't move.

"It's all love," they say. "It's over, young buck! You did it."

I keep going . . . keep swinging like my life depends on it.

Later, Scoop tells me my heart is bigger than my chest.

"One more Code. Fifteen: Protect yourself at all times."

Scoop puts a .22-caliber Beretta in my palm.

It's heavy in my hands. I marvel at it. I feel like Pac in *Juice* or maybe Pacino in *Scarface*. Nino in *New Jack*. Everybody else but me. I wonder if I can use this in my nightmares, use it to blow back evil. I think about the cops, the robber, the repo man. Fear melts in the palm of my hand.

I'm a lyrical destructor, don't make me buck ya
Because I'm a wild muhfucka*

"Is it loaded?"
"No use otherwise."

* "Give Up the Goods," Big Noyd (Mobb Deep featuring Big Noyd), 1995.

17

Some Type of Way

My stomach feels like a dishrag. Tongue like a balloon in my mouth. Eyes unbuttoned. Jaw weeping. Even the sky bleeds as the sun sets over Nia's crib. She lives on Stenton Ave. across the street from MLK High School.

"But why?" she asks me, patting my face with an ice pack. I'm in her room. It's baby blue and has stuffed animals all over her bed like *Jumanji*.

"'Cause," I say slow.

"'Cause what?" She wipes my face.

I don't know what to say. I don't even know why. Maybe I did it because Uzi's gone and UPK are like my big brothers now. Or because Amir wanted to do it too. Or for protection. Or to piss Pops off. Or because I just don't give a fuck anymore. Or maybe there is no why.

"'Cause, whatever."

She just shakes her head. "They beat you up. What type of—"

"Nah, we got jumped in, plus we fucked them up too."

"I guess," she says, rolling her eyes, "I don't see the point if they're supposed to be your friends."

Nia is like fresh water. She has me feeling some type of way.

"You love that bitch?" Ryan asked me the other day.

I almost ripped his head off. "She ain't no bitch. Chill with that . . . and yeah, I'm feelin her, so fall back."

I just stare at her, stare at her like she's the most precious piece of artwork in the Philly Museum of Art. Her skin is silky and shiny like the outside of a bubble. Each one of her eyelashes shows and curls into forever.

"Look at your little peach fuzz," she says, laughing, touching my bruised chin. She has a smile that stops at nothing.

Her mom's at work—she's all mine.

She kisses me, her lips softer than a whisper. I can feel my heart beating in my dick, stone stiff. My hands take over like they're possessed. I play her collarbone like a harmonica.

We fuck like our lives depend on it, like we're all we have, and I think it's true.

We're lying on her bed, watching the ceiling fan make circles in the dark. Her neck, smooth and warm, resting on my bicep in perfect tilt.

"What's the craziest thing you ever did?" I ask her.

Her eyes roll back in thought.

"I know."

"What?"

"Fall in love with you."

"But you don't even know me like that to be falling in love."

"I know," she says, getting back on top of me. "That's why it's so crazy . . . Did you know that love causes the same chemical reaction in the brain as insanity?"

I think about that for a minute—love and insanity, beauty and the beast.

"Crazy."

18
MALO

Scoop hands me a frosty forty of OE. I hit it, then put it on my swollen face like an ice pack. It's all big and awkward, like a traffic cone.

I look down 5th Street: little girls with braids and colorful Venus Williams barrettes jumping rope fast. Little boys juking in the middle of the street, playing roughhouse, shooting at a bottomless black crate tied to a phone pole. Sirens whine in the distance.

"Yo! What you call a pretty girl on Ryan's arm?" Amir asks.

"I don't fuckin know."

"A tattoo! Haha."

"Ya mom!" Ryan says. He's sitting between this girl Tasha's legs, getting his hair braided.

I kiss my mama goodbye and wipe the tears from her lonely eyes
Said I'll return but I gotta fight the fate's arrived*

This Cambodian kid, Dah, is tatting my arm up. Dah's my age and can make a tattoo gun out of an electric toothbrush, Bic pen, and guitar string. He's doing it right now—sharpening the guitar string against the mouth of the curb like floss. Dah is like Uptown's MacGyver. Give homie some duct tape, a couple of paper clips, batteries, a tube sock, and like two and a half hours, and he'll make a better version of anything they sell at Radio Shack. Once he even made a bulletproof vest out of Kevlar strips he ganked from some old Goodyears.

Everyone comes to Dah to get tatted, twenty bucks a lick. He put a crucifix on Ted's veiny-ass forearm, "Only God Can Judge Me" on Aubrey's back, "MOB" on D-Rock's hand, a teardrop under Scoop's eye, and two cherries on Amber's left titty, and he did way too many RIP tats.

"I use the E string 'cause it's mad thin," he says, his dark anime eyes bugged with focus. "Can also straighten staples for the needle, but I like the E. It plays music on nghz' skin."

"Dah, you ain't a ngh, stop saying ngh, ngh," D-Rock says.

"Eat a dick," Dah says, "ngh."

D-Rock's just fucking with Dah. Nobody cares that Dah says ngh because—forreal-forreal—Dah and all the other Cambodians in Olney are nghz. They look like nghz—dark, thick features; dress like nghz—baggy and colorful; talk like nghz—fast and raw; and are even broker than nghz, with like forty people in a two-bedroom apartment. They don't own shit—no nail salons, no beauty stores, no laundromats, no

* "I Ain't Mad At Cha," 2Pac featuring Danny Boy, 1996.

check-cashing spots, no corner stores, no banks, no take-out spots with cloudy bulletproof glass—just like nghz. I think the other Asians look down on them too . . . just like nghz.

"It hurts like a bitch," Amir says, biting open a grape freeze pop.

"It's the real ngh way. No shop, no license," Ted says. "Just needle to bone."

I don't care, though. I hope it hurts. That jump-in plus everything else with my fam got me numb to pain. I can take it, bring it. I don't feel shit, cold as steel.

"Aight!" Dah says as he tapes it all together and inspects it.

"Damn, that shit is ugly," D-Rock, says staring at Dah's invention. It has a medieval body and a jailhouse spirit.

"Looks ain't everything—like a bad bitch could have that house in Virginia, you never know," says Scoop.

"Essaywhuman?" I say like Black Thought from the Roots.

"HIV, ngh!"

D-Rock, Scoop, and Aubrey are chilling. Blunt smoke slow-dances around their faces. The door to Scoop's tinted-out gold Benz is ajar. Biggie pours out of the Pioneers. D-Rock is draining a Keystone Light.

"Man, all y'all nghz shut the fuck up and throw something up," Ted says, taking his shirt off fast like he's about to rumble.

"Go 'head with all that lifting shit, man."

"You ain't lifting, you ain't living!" he barks. "I'ma show y'all simple nghz how I'm living." He starts doing reps on the bench. He woofs like a dog every time he throws the weight up. And that's exactly what Ted reminds me of: a little hyper pug dog, always drooling at the corners of the mouth, always wild, ready to scrap, loud as fuck. Uzi says he has a Napoleon complex.

Dah bangs the gun against the curb.

"That jawn still works, right?" I ask, laughing. Dah just looks at me, mouth twisted, head tilted.

"What? Name one thing I made that didn't work," he challenges.

I thought about the bulletproof vest he made since—

"And don't say the vest!"

Last year, this kid Edris, one of Uzi's best boys, bought Dah's bulletproof vest. He was rocking it, and on his way home from some girl's house, right there in front of the laundromat on Broad Street—Wishy Washy—they ambushed him. The vest stopped a few slugs from wreaking havoc on his chest, but it was useless above his linebacker shoulders. Shells shatter skull. They went point-blank and shot his nose off like the Sphinx. It's crazy how many people are getting killed throughout the city. Every night someone's son or daughter is murdered and it seems like nobody cares. Death feels like it's around every corner, waiting under the stop signs, looking down from the street lights, creeping out of the sewers.

"They took the elevator on him—top floor. It was a bulletproof vest, not mask," Dah says. "The vest worked," he adds, hitting a switch on the tattoo gun, which suddenly buzzes to life, "and so does this . . . ready?"

Dah's passionate about what he does. I think it's dope to

see people who are passionate do their thing, like MJ—either one. Plus out here all you got is your name. That's exactly why I'm getting my name tatted on me.

"Hell yeah," I say, and take off my shirt. "I want *Malo* right here," pointing to my whole left arm. "Big as shit. Loud. All the way turned up."

"Got you." He writes it out—*MALO*—on a piece of paper in Old English letters. The letters are sharp curves like ninja stars. As I'm staring at my name it hits me that there are two types of people: camels and lions. Camels—the ones that follow and always do as they're told, listen quietly and never question, never challenge. Those that bend every which way to please the world, the authorities, parents, school, government, and follow blindly. Lions—the ones that make their own rules, chart their own path. The lions are the G's and the camels are the bustas. It's like Scoop always says: "G's do what they want, bustas do what they can."

I shoot up like a rocket.

"What?" Dah says.

"You know how Tupac said *THUG LIFE* stands for 'The Hate U Gave Little Infants Fucks Everybody'?"

"Yeah."

"*MALO*—'Me Against Law and Order.'"

19

Can't Stop, Won't Stop

Roach is chasing me down the hallway, limping after me like a hungry pirate. He's the shape of a sack of laundry—a stuttering hamper coming right at me. I don't even know why he's chasing me or what I did this time. I just decide to run, so now I'm running, fast like how my dad says my great-great-grandfather ran when he escaped slavery in Valdosta. It's not even lunch yet and the Limp is after me. *Feets, don't fail me now.*

The BS starts in chemistry.

I get there and teacher Helga is in my ass like a bike with no seat.

"Where were you?" she asks like the police. Her face drags and drips like an old melted candle.

I just shrug. She doesn't know what's going on with my family. Doesn't want to know either. Plus I'm not telling my whole life story in front of the class.

She keeps pushing. "Well?"

"Well what?"

"Detention," she says.

"Do what you gotta do," I say.

She notices my rolled-up sleeve. I'm wearing my fresh tat like a Purple Heart. It's big and raised like it's in 3-D.

"See, class?" she announces to everyone. "You'll go nowhere in life with that thing on your arm. Nowhere!"

Written in school textbooks, Bibles, et cetera.
Fuck a school lecture, the lies get me vexed-er*

She gets back to the class, lecturing us about substances that can't be broken down into any other substance.

"Helmets, helmets," she keeps saying in her thick German accent. Her voice is always harsh and angry. I laugh. She means "elements."

What's the point? My hands are in my pocket rubbing lint. I'm broke. Mom's broke. Dad's broke. Uzi's broken.

"Can you teach us how to make money?" I ask with my hand up.

"No. This is chemistry."

"You said that chemistry came from alchemy . . . and alchemy is turning base metals like copper and lead into precious metals like silver and gold . . . turning something into nothing . . . how do you turn rabbit ears into fat pockets?"

"Stop talking right now." She points at me.

Nothing they teach here is useful—just a bunch of stuff to memorize and spit back, like this is karaoke night. I don't see

* "One Love," Nas, 1994.

the point. Maybe it's like the whole camels-and-lions thing. Maybe this is where they train the camels to follow blindly. Tests, tests, and more tests, that's the only language they speak. Fuck their test. Life is my test.

I'm tagging in my notebook when I hear his voice in the hallway.

"Where's Milu?" I hear him ask. He can never say my name right. Why? It's not that hard—*Malo* (ma-low)—plus I hear this muhfucka say way harder names perfectly. He never fucks up *Tsyplakov* (sip-lih-kov) or *Rydzewski* (rid-zes-key) or *Ruotsalainen* (roo-aht-suh-li-nen). Fuck is so hard about *Malo*?

I don't even know why he's looking for me. I never know.

I slide out of the back door and into the hallway. He buzzes across my sight. Beelines toward me.

"Milu! Come!" he yells at my back like I'm Lassie. I might turn into Cujo on his bitch ass. I act like I don't hear him—he didn't call my name anyway.

I run down the hallway, book bags scattered along the sides like sandbags. All eyes on me. I slap all the open lockers shut. This school has mad hiding spots and I know them all. I've used them all before.

Random classroom—

Posters of dead white dudes—Washington, Adams, Jefferson—stare down at me as I hide. They grit on me like the judge gritted on Uzi in Arizona.

—

Storage closet—

Crystal finds me in here. Kianna calls Crystal a "fast-ass lil' skeezer." She's my age but she's always messing with older guys. She flashes me and I feel her up until Bobby, the janitor, old black dude with a pimp stroll, barges in. "Give me five on the black hand side," he says to me, then tells us "to get the hell outta here."

Bathroom—

I find my boy Jessie in here. He's mixed, lives with his white mom and grandma, who are both cool as shit. He writes graffiti and has a name all over West Philly. I wish he was in my grade but he's in high school. He pulls out a silver Sharpie and we bomb the stalls. He tells me about all the rappers who write graf.

"Fat Joe writes *Crack*. Masta Ace writes *Ase*. Havoc from Mobb Deep writes *Nal*. Bushwick Bill writes *Spade*. Fab 5 Freddy writes *Spin*."

Jessie writes *JesOne*. Me: *MALO*. They'll never forget my name.

I got twenty-five cans in my knapsack, crossin out the wick-wack
Puttin up my name with a fat cap*

On the roof—

Bird's-eye of Philly. Dirty gray sky pushes down on me from above. Down below the city waits to swallow me up, its big mouth open wide like it's yawning.

* "Out for Fame," KRS-One, 1995.

—

I keep running. In the hallway, I bump into Fred. He's standing there with Flynn, this rich white kid who's always wearing bow ties and boat shoes and who likes to laugh and make fun of the starving African kids in the Feed the Children commercials—punk ass. Fred is mixed, black and white, and we go way back. Back in elementary we used to kill the talent shows. We were Kris Kross, had the whole school like "Jump, Jump" in our backward Phillies and Sixers jerseys, hair twisted up with little black rubber bands. We did the Kid 'n Play too, dancing, rocking the crowd like *House Party*. But now he hangs with these corny-ass kids. He fronts like he doesn't know me, doesn't know my mom, my dad, my bro, like we didn't spend weekends together playing in North Philly or Mt. Airy, like we never had love. Fred laughs when his new friends talk shit about black people like he's not half black. Fuck it, no time to think about that right now.

"Shhhhh . . . don't say anything," is the only thing I say as I run past him. As soon as Fred sees me, then Roach, I hear him blurt out: "He went that way, Principal!"

At the end of the hallway, the end of the road, a dead end. My back against the big brown doors that sound like trucks when they open. Roach's a few feet away. I push the doors open with my butt.

"If you leave, don't come back," he says.

The brown trucks give one last honk as I burst out into daylight and keep running.

Dear Carole,

The crowd of "friends" around me disappears after Chaka leaves. Every now and then Malo says, "So-and-so said to say hello." I ask him, "Why didn't you tell me that you saw so-and-so?" His response is, "They know your number." It sounds cold to me but it's true. If they want to talk to me, they can pick up the phone or drop me a note. Some of them try. But truth be told, I don't want to hear from anyone. Why would I?

Who are these people and what are they to me? How do they see me and in whose image? The platitudes and praises are gone but I knew this. "Don't take it seriously," I remember telling myself. "There is an agenda behind those flowery words." Malo has always taken everyone with a grain of salt. At his young age, he knows bullshit. He wants no part of it. He knows how to hide his disdain, but doesn't.

They expect me to keel over and wither. They expect me to howl at the moon. They expect me to beseech and plead, to cower and beg, to grovel and bend. I'm dying a little inside but they don't know who I am: the little girl from Brooklyn that can throw down with the best of them. I'm in survival mode and it's taking all of the energy I have.

I'm in survival mode and everyone and everything that crosses my path has to bow to that energy. Even my dreams are in survival mode. "What doesn't kill you makes you stronger!" I wonder who said that. It might be true but all of this was killing ground. It was a matter of when and where. The killing ground was the given and I know it all too well. Survive and the ground won't swallow you!

Survive and the fear won't envelop you! Survive and the next day the horizon appears just as you thought you were breathing your last breath. I know something about life and death. I can't embrace life the way that many people do but I know how to survive.

So it's no surprise when the company disappears and the phone calls stop. On chance meetings at a store or on the street, they examine me intensely, looking for "damage." I smile inside. The "damage" you are looking for has always been there. What you are seeing now is "survival."

God, give me strength.

Amina

20

C.R.E.A.M.

The root of evil isn't money, it's not having money. Brokeness blows dark thoughts into my mind like thick black smoke. The worst part is seeing my mom suffer. It weighs on me, clings to me like wet clothes.

Criminal minded you've been blinded . . .

The other night, riding 'round the city with Scoop and Amir, I peep what this whole world is about. It's as clear as a Ziploc that cash—bucks, endz, dough, bread, scratch, cheese, loot, green, gwop, bank—rules everything around me, near me, in the distance, and on the hazy horizon. I think about all the songs about money: "Get Money," "For the Love of $," "C.R.E.A.M.," "All for the Money," "Dead Presidents," "Paid in Full," "It All Comes Down to the Money," "Mo Money, Mo Problems," "Money, Power, Respect," "Money Money

Money." About how all the artists that made those songs probably felt like I feel right now.

Visualizin the realism of life and actuality
Fuck who's the baddest a person's status depends on salary*

I see how the jawns react to bread. Like this one girl, Jade, gorgeous thick dime jawn from Nicetown. She's older, like eighteen. One day I try to rap to her on the C bus, approach her all respectful, and she just igs me like I'm not even there. Then this other day I'm riding through her hood in Scoop's bug-eyed Benz and she spots me, flags me down like I'm a taxi. I barely have to speak, she just hops in and starts giving me head in the whip like I'm Joe Pesci in *Casino*. Later on she tells me, "Nghz are like bank accounts. Without money, they don't generate interest."

Far as I can see, money buys everything: hoes, cars, clothes, land, even freedom. Uzi's only in jail because we don't have the money to keep him out. At Uzi's sentencing, cracka-ass judge spent more time talking about fines and money and restitutions and penalties and paybacks and fees than anything else. Shit is a racket. Everybody's getting paid: the lawyers, the judges, the guards, the cops, the old chick with the glasses typing, all the companies making the uniforms, the handcuffs, the shackles. Everybody's banking—everybody except us.

* "Life's a Bitch," AZ (Nas featuring AZ), 1994.

—

I'm about to change that, though. I'm fifteen now, man of the house, and it's time to make my own way. America is about the golden rule: those with the gold make the rules. I'm getting my own gold. It's like that Billie Holiday song my mom used to play around the house: *God bless the child that's got his own, that's got his own*. It's on me. My mom is already stressed out enough, I'm not going to make it worse by asking her for money. I want to give her one less thing to worry about. I don't want to ask my pops. He's cheap and probably doesn't have it anyway. Plus—fuck asking. Asking means strings attached, means owing, and I don't owe nobody. I feel like I'm alone anyway.

Where did my family go? What happened to us?

The day has come. Time to get my hustle on. Fashion trends are always changing, but getting money is a style that never plays out. The hustle runs through my blood like diabetes.

Bone presses a code to unlock a door to a secret storage room in his basement. Everything is dark, smoky, shadowy. Duffle bags, scales, baggies. Barking, howling, pacing pits and Rots with wet fangs guard the gates to the Garden of Weeden. The basement is dark with low ceilings. Bone is short with hair all over his face like the Lebanese dudes that own all the sneaker stores on Market Street. He's got a blue Phillies fitted over his eyes.

"I get everything," he says. "Blueberry Kush, Super Skunk, Sour Diesel, White Widow, Maui Wowie, Blue Sky, Afghan Kush, Acapulco Gold, Holland's Hope, G-13, Jedi Kush, Northern Lights, Panama Red, Purple Haze, Quebec Gold, Three Kings, everything." Bone moves more trees than Timberland. "All my shit is KB, kine bud. *Kine* basically means 'the shit' in Hawaiian."

People around my way are used to dirt weed, that brown brick catnip shit from Mexico that smells like feet and doesn't really get you high, just gives you a sleepy headache, and has more seeds and stems than Fairmount Park. Some grimy dealers spray their dirt with Raid ant killer and try to call it exotic.

My plan is to bring Bone's shit back around my way and make a killing.

I got advice from my father, all he told me was this
Ngh, get off your ass if you plan to be rich*

I know Bone through Amir, and Amir knows him through Damien. Damien is this fat black boy from South Philly who lives with Bone, they're like brothers. He's also the hatchet man, the bodyguard, down to do dirt. Amir tells me that Damien killed somebody who owed Bone a hundred bucks, just off principle.

We walk into the main room and Damien starts talking shit, first on Amir, then on me, then Bone:

"Amir so black he bleeds smoke.

"Malo, your head looks like Mt. Rushmore . . . Your hats and haircuts should cost extra.

* "Blasphemy," 2pac, 1996.

"Doesn't Bone look like a retarded albino Chihuahua?"

The whole time Amir is just shaking his head, trying not to laugh. Then Amir slowly rises to his feet for his stand-up:

"Damien, you so ugly, when you smile your face hurts.

"You so fat you livin large.

"Look at your hairline, Damien, it's pushed so far back I can read your damn mind.

"Damien's so fat he got arrested for having twenty pounds of *crack*!"

Everybody laughs except Bone, who takes me back into the stash room. He weighs out three ounces on a digital scale.

"You got three things," he says. "Good, fast, and cheap . . . but you can only have two at any given time. So if it's fast and cheap, it ain't good. If it's good and cheap, it ain't fast." He hands me the work. "This right here: fast and good . . . not cheap."

Dear Carole,

Philadelphia public schools are notorious in many ways and I need to protect Malo as much as I can. Malo has been stoic throughout all of this but I wonder what is going on with him inside.

My mind is on the future and determining what school Malo will attend. Education for me was always the key and I assumed that my sons would feel the same way. After all, African Americans have made great strides but we still have so far to go. That is my dream for my children but reality is seeping in as they let me know in many different ways that they don't want to follow. Like Daudi, Malo was expelled from the seventh grade. And like Daudi, he has picked up on the thug life. My sons love the hood and its most material aspects. He is wilding out. He smokes weed and drinks. He seems most concerned with hanging out and doesn't want to spend any energy on his future right now. He is angry with me and I understand that.

I understand Malo's need to explore and test the boundaries. I rebelled in a different way but I definitely rebelled. But as someone who grew up in the hood, I am all too aware of its dangers and peril, especially for young black men. It will sort itself out but I know that this precipice that they are on could drop from underneath them and then the journey is over.

I want to protect Malo most at a time when he least wants to be protected. I want to be close to him when he wants to be as far away from me as possible. I sense the perils that hover over him and smell the excitement and the adventures that await him. My sons are dear to me. Daudi with his maddening, manic behavior and Malo with his sly, confident moves are a part of me.

I hug Malo but my mind is on the future. How is it that the future has become so tenuous for both of my sons and, truth be told, me?

God, give me strength.

Amina

21

G-Town

Me and my mom move to the twelfth floor of this building in Germantown that my mom calls a "concrete monstrosity." My old neighborhood, in Olney, wasn't the ghetto. It had its ghetto parts with drugs and shootings like everywhere in Philly, but my block was nice and our crib was a big brown and white Tudor house. But this new spot in G-Town is the ghetto for real. Our building looks like Tracy Towers, the building where my cousins stay at in the Bronx, and Tracy Towers looks like the building from *Good Times*. *Ain't we lucky we got 'em.*

And like Tracy Towers, our building has an incinerator for trash. My mom tells me where it is and hands me a plastic CVS bag full of trash. I walk across the hall to the little incinerator room. It's warm and smells like the steam from manholes. I grab the metal handle and pull open the shaft. I can feel the heat from below. I put the bag in the chute, close it, and listen to our trash fall, crash, and burn.

I didn't want to move here, but fuck it, I'm never home, so it doesn't really matter where I live, I guess. It's like Uzi said: "I'm a Nomadic Addict Merchant." Anyway, it's probably a good thing. I think my mom needs to get away from our old crib, too many memories. Too much pain living in those old walls.

Our new walls are paper thin, absorbing the voices, noises, and lives of the people living above, below, on both sides, and across from us—box life.

Germantown is still Uptown Philly, it's like a ten-minute ride from Olney. It's blacker than Olney, though. In Olney, you got everybody—Cambodians, Indians, Russians, Puerto Rocks, Caribbeans, blacks, whites—on some United Nations shit. G-Town is basically all black except for the people that own the blur of sneaker, beauty, and liquor stores and the bail bond, check-cashing, and tax return spots and the Chinese food, Chicago, Louisiana, Kentucky, New York, and Hollywood Fried Chicken joints. Other than that it's all black.

We live on the twelfth floor. From the terrace, everyone below looks like little commas. Rooftops bright with hanging laundry and satellite dishes. At night, police choppers, ghetto birds—vultures—fly around with their thirsty searchlights crawling up the walls, flooding the night.

It's cold. The heat in our apartment isn't working, so I pull the oven open.

The walls in my room are naked white and I ain't putting no clothes on this cave bitch. No posters, no pictures, no shit to remember or to live by, no nothing. Who knows how long I'll be here?

I'm older now, see what having a father's about
One day they can be in your life, next day they be out*

My mom tells me I got a letter from my dad. I'm still too mad at him to open it. I just add it to the pile. When Amir comes over to see our new spot, he peeps the stack.

"These all from your dad?" he asks, thumbing through the envelopes.

"Yeah."

"You ain't open none of 'em?" he says, face scrunched in confusion.

"I don't fuck with him like that. Not after what he did." Every time I think about my dad, I see him leaving, hear my mom crying, and feel Uzi screaming in the cage.

"Man, at least you got a pop. At least he's trying. Nobody's perfect but at least you can talk to him, at least he wants to talk to you." He stares through me, his eyes burning into mine. Amir has never met his dad even though they live in the same neighborhood. "You know what I'd do to get a letter from my dad? A phone call? An acknowledgment? Anything, anything!"

Amir takes off his chain.

"See this?" He flashes it, then throws it to me. The chain is silver and flat with a charm on the end.

* "Poppa Was a Playa," Nas, 1998.

"That was my dad's. It's the only thing he left." The charm is a symbol I've seen somewhere before but can't place it. It kind of looks like a *W* with too many loops and arrow points at the top. Maybe it's another language?

The next time my pop calls, I pick up. I don't know what the fuck to say. I want to hang up.

"Come stay with your father a few nights . . . in Levittown."

"Levittown?" I say after a while. *Where the hell is that?* There is so much I want to say but I don't want to show him how hurt I am. "That sounds far."

"It's not that far from Philly, depending on traffic. About forty-five minutes."

"Forty-five minutes? Might as well live in Jersey."

"Well, it's actually right on the border. This area was built after the war by Levitt and Sons. They wouldn't sell to black people. The first black people to move into this neighborhood, Bill and Daisy Myers, in 1957 . . . I think it was '57 . . . they moved to Dogwood Hollow. People threw rocks and Molotov cocktails at their house, drove by and screamed 'nigger' and 'porch monkey,' bomb threats. They stayed in Levittown, though, stuck it out. They called Daisy Myers the Rosa Parks of the North."

"You moved out there because of all that?"

"No. I thought I should get out of the city . . . and this is all I could afford. But let's talk about this face-to-face. I want to see you."

"Nah, I gotta stay here. Somebody's gotta watch after Mom. She's sick, remember?"

"Let me come pick you up. We can talk."

"Nah," I say, ice cold.

"Why?" he asks.

"You made your bed. Lie in it."

Dear Carole,

I am sure that Malo is selling weed or something! How can I say that so calmly? My calm is actually tenuously sitting on a very stormy sea and one more huge wave can knock the two of us into the water, never to come up again. I tried to give Malo some money and he told me not to worry—he had money, and if I needed money, he would give me some. I just looked at him. I heard what he was saying and I could see his mouth move but I couldn't comprehend that this child had his own money. He is fiercely independent.

I'm not afraid for him just as I wasn't afraid for myself when at a younger age than Malo I rolled a drunk's pocket in the hallway of my apartment building on Cooper Street in Brooklyn. He was there for the taking and I with no money saw him lying there and I could hear the jingle of coins in his pockets. He would mumble a few words every now and then but he was basically out of commission. Where did I even get the notion to roll him? I honestly don't know. But I did just that. I was able to get a few dollars and thought no more about it.

I never asked Malo if he was selling weed but I know and I also know that the ground beneath us has gone asunder.

Malo doesn't know what tomorrow will bring now that his father has left. He doesn't trust the state that I am in or will be in. And why should he? His father was a constant. Not because he was always at home but because he had always been on the road, and when he wasn't on the road he was always at the office, and when he wasn't at the office he was always cheerful. "Wake up in joy" was his expression in the morning. He didn't have to be hospitalized and he wasn't sad and he didn't take medicine for depression, so despite his chronic absences from Malo's childhood, he was a known equation.

I, on the other hand, represented the mercurial, the artiste, the reclusive, and the unknown. Perhaps Chaka had spoken to Malo about my "condition." I don't know. I am the parent that is there but not there. Chaka was away but he wasn't away. At least that is what everyone likes to think.

My mother called me a thief. She said if there was one thing that she couldn't stand, it was a "thief and a liar." I was both. I stole because I had to. My mother seemed oblivious to our plight, so I had to do something about it. My mother felt that honesty somehow trumped poverty and that we could hold on to honesty even when we were hungry. I didn't buy that line and was angry with my mother for a long time because of that.

I stole food from the corner store until they caught me and told me never to come in the store again. I stole food. After Ben and Irving (that was the name of the store owners) banned me from the store, I sent my brother to go "get" food for us. I stole from my aunt. I would wait for her to go to sleep and then I would roll her. She snored heavily and that was my signal to go into her purse and take some money. Unlike my mother, she always had a little money on her. During the day she carried her money in her bra but there was always a few dollars in her purse. I never took everything and tried to take an amount that she wouldn't miss. Eventually I was caught and had to pay my aunt back but the worst part was my mother's scorn: "I don't care how smart you are, if you are a liar and a thief, you will never be any good." The ironic part is that my aunt took advantage of my mother and our situation for years. She didn't have a problem cheating us and there wasn't anyone to call her out on this.

There was a time when I stole the rent money from a family that lived right behind us. I can still see them. There was a mother and father in that apartment so that stuck out. I was back there playing with the kids and somehow I noticed the envelope with the rent money. Now this was a lot of money. It was around ninety dollars. I took the entire envelope. This was serious business and I felt it. I remember their grief at "losing" the money and how everyone was looking for the money. They never suspected me and I don't know why they didn't. This was a terrible move on my part. First of all, it was really more money than I could handle. It took me forever to spend it and I ended up giving some of it away and my aunt cheated me out of the rest. Secondly, they moved shortly afterward and I always felt responsible for that.

My mother got wind that I had some money and of course she asked me about it. I wasn't going to tell her where the money came from. A constant threat in my home was the juvenile detention center, where liars and thieves were sent if they continued to misbehave. My aunt stepped up to the plate and said that the money was hers.

Now I knew that was a lie but there was nothing that I could say. So my aunt was the lucky recipient of my ill-gotten goods and I was on punishment once again. Things are never what they seem. I believe that my mother knew that my aunt was a liar and a cheat but she depended on my aunt emotionally and in some ways financially. I think that my mother's super-piousness stemmed from an imaginary place that placed an extraordinary value on being "good."

Malo isn't in the exact place that I was but he is in a place that has him thinking for the first time in his life about survival. I understand that and I trust him but I don't want him selling weed.

God, give me strength.

Amina

22

Trouble in Paradise

I hit up Twin Gold on Fifth Street to buy a fourteen-karat white gold tennis bracelet for Nia. She didn't ask for it. It's not her birthday or anything, I just want to do something nice for her. I give it to her and her eyes light up. Then they get dim. She puts two and two together and asks me straight up if I'm selling.

"Don't ask too many questions and I won't tell you no lies," I say, laughing. I forget where I heard that. She's not laughing, though.

"I'm getting money." I pull out a knot as thick as a pocket Bible, trying to impress her. "That's all that matters."

"That's not all that matters, Malo! You know where you're going to end up doing that."

"Where?"

"Dead or in jail."

"Look," putting my money away, "I need a girl to blow my mind, not my high. You know how many—"

"What? How many girls are easily impressed? I'm not them. Money doesn't impress me. Everything isn't about money." There's something refreshing about that but I'm not trying to hear that right now.

"Yeah? Like what isn't?"

"Love, my love for you . . . do you know what that means? Love?" I think about love. I do love Nia but haven't told her yet. I shrug.

"Love is learning the song in someone's heart and singing it to them when they forget, forget who they are, forget where their brother already is."

I try to kiss her—

"Don't."

She gives me an ultimatum: her or hustlin.

My palms itch, I can feel the money coming.

My heart hurts, I can feel Nia leaving.

My soul cries, I feel death calling.

I choose the hustle.

Dear Carole,

The people who were always around during my marriage left without a goodbye. They didn't leave really, they disappeared. One day they were there and then they were gone. In their absence, I survive. In their absence, I pull in the night and walk with the day. In their absence, I don't suffer fools and prophets. Instead, I listen to the silence. In their absence, the silence whispers and then shouts and I listen. In their absence, I learn the meaning of one. In their absence, I cry without tears and sound but cry just the same. In their absence, I stand for fear of what would happen if I lie down. In their absence, I remember how I used to play.

Double Dutch was my game and I was good at it. I loved the competitive nature of it and winning brought me great pleasure and attention. The older girls let me jump with them, and the rope became a safe haven for me. "All, all, all in together now, how do you like the weather now . . ." I knew how to play. I could remember "scaling" fences and how exhilarated it made me feel to be able to go over the fence without touching it with my legs. I knew how to play. I knew how to play stoopball. I loved handball although my brother always beat me at it. I drove my sister's bike until I almost ran over a little girl and the father said to me, "You are too big to be riding a bike!" Is that what he meant to say? I was thirteen or fourteen. I lived on Georgia Avenue then. I stopped riding Maggie's bike after that and it was stolen shortly after that. Who told me I couldn't have fun? I know how to play.

God, give me strength.

Amina

23

The Greek

Ryan's gun in my grill.

"Don't point that shit at me," I say, pushing him away. He tilts the piece in my direction—this way, that way, like he's selling it to me. Morning light bounces off black steel.

"Fuck you say about my mama?" he says like O-Dog from the opening scene in *Menace II Society*. He stands, points the tool in the air, and flashes a smirk.

"You feel sorry for who?" he says, and moves closer.

"I don't want any trouble," I say like the Korean shopkeeper. "Just get out!"

Blal! Blal! Blal! He punches the gun sideways and I can almost hear gunshots. *Blal! Blal! Blal!*

"Where's the motherfuckin videotape? Give me the motherfuckin videotape . . . Stop, bring yo . . ." *Blal! Blal!*

"Hey, ngh. Clean the cash register. Come on," he says, and sprints out of my room laughing. He comes back in with a big smile on his face. "Today is the day," he says. "The Greek. Get up! Time to ride out."

The Greek is this festival where everybody goes buck. A Carolina-blue sky hangs over West Phil. The thermometer above the PSFS bank on Girard Ave. says it's 101 degrees. We pull up to the Greek like Mad Max, zooming over cobblestones and trolley tracks on ATVs.

I'm on a black Yamaha Banshee four-wheeler with chrome pipes, hitting the throttle and making it growl like a Harley. *Vhm-vhm-vhm-vhm-vhm-vhmmmmm*. Ryan is on a Banshee too, blue and yellow, with a cocaine-white T-shirt wrapped around his head like some Saudi oil sheik. Amir and Kam are on dirt bikes. Then there's the extended fam, other crews on all types of off-road shit. Big tees flapping in the wind as we weave up Girard Ave. through parking-lot-pace traffic. We ride into the Plateau and chill on a hill overlooking the festival.

Out in Philly we be up in the parks
A place called the Plateau is where everybody go*

The park is jumping, the most people I've seen in one place since my pops took me to the Million Man March, the last place I remember chilling with my dad, just me and him, and a million other brothers. I remember Farrakhan saying: "We want to bring you back to Washington with your wives . . . because the new century must be the century of family. With-

* "Summertime," DJ Jazzy Jeff and the Fresh Prince, 1998.

out strong family you don't have strong community or a strong nation. We must rebuild the black family."

I guess we ain't going back to Washington.

The Greek isn't about black family, it's about black freaks. Hot boys stuntin, fly girls struttin, everybody showin out. Girls, every shade of brown, colorful as feathers, brush by looking like queens, stars, models, video vixens, hood rats, and hot-ass messes. They cut across my sight with big phat donkey butts switching in every direction. Crayola hair colors. Daisy Dukes cut as tight as bikinis. D cups fall into the dope boy whips: 600 Benzes with AMG kits, 5-Series Beamers, Mazzies, Lambos, Rostas, Raris, Double R's.

Banging girls with skin like shiny marble. Diesel dudes shove by with cobras and boa constrictors around their necks like gold chains. Shorts and Timbs. Polo sweats with one leg up. Jerseys: Iverson, Kidd, Bryant, Jordan. Mecca, FUBU, Maurice Malone, Pelle Pelle, Enyce, Ice Berg, Moschino, Versace, Lo. Lowriders with hydraulics and juicy paint jobs, cruising on three wheels, hitting switches like mad scientists. Dudes with canes, dancing with arms out. Pink, yellow, purple biker shorts. Herringbones. Bathing suits. Bandanas. Some girls dancing on top of cars. Washcloths on top of their domes. Drinking bottles of beer. Wet T-shirt contest. Junk trunks. Booty shake shake-offs. Hot dogs and burgers on the grill. Even white girls out here, the kind with wraps and gold chains, white chocolate.

Anything goes out here. Guys film up girls' skirts. Girls whip their titties out like badges—flash. Dudes pulling their dicks out, flashing girls. Every few minutes—a roaring outbreak. Thirsty guys with camcorders getting girls in booty shorts to go buck.

"Take yo shirt off . . . Let me see something . . . Pull 'em out . . ." Hands grabbing whatever they can.

"Stop . . . Move . . . Get away ngh . . ." They run through an endless tunnel of pinchers, cuppers, cuffers, palmers, grabbers. Asses bouncing everywhere like a Snoop video. Dudes splash water on chicks like it's champagne and they just won the championship. "Pussy," someone says. We turn to see a girl with a short-ass skirt and no panties. Fifty dudes swarming her, video cameras pointed every which way like the paparazzi. A circle with popping pussies and asses in the center.

The crowd moves to South Street and I think about Odunde, this summertime African festival on South Street that my dad took me to back in the day. I remember all the people, the families, smiling, dancing, eating, laughing, posing for photos. I remember how my dad would give me ten bucks and I'd bargain with the vendors. Then we'd follow this procession led by stilt dancers in African masks with drums and shekeres and stop at the South Street bridge overlooking the Schuylkill River.

From the street, we would watch the priest and priestess, dressed in white robes, stand over the bridge singing African hymns, dancing, and throwing flowers into the river.

"They're making an offering to Oshun," I remember my dad telling me. "Oshun is the unseen mother present at every gathering. She is the goddess of the river. The Yoruba say that no one is an enemy to water and therefore everyone must respect Oshun." The crowd joins the white robes and catches the spirit, chanting and shaking.

"The Yoruba say that when she possesses her followers, she dances, flirts, and then weeps."

"Weeps? Why?" I said, thinking about my mom.

"Weeps because no one can love her enough and the world is not as beautiful as she knows it could be."

Night falls hard.

Me, Amir, and Scoop hit up Club McDonald's on Broad and Susquehanna. Most of the people who were at the park earlier are now out here in front of Mickey D's. Steam shoots up from manholes. Scuffles, commotion, little rumbles break out around us. Scoop is thirsty for drama. He's mean-mugging everybody, pushing nghz, and instigating fights.

The Ruff Riders crew zooms back and forth on Kawasakis, tires burning rubber and spinning smoke in the street. They put on a show, busting out long seat-scraping-street wheelies while they stand up, sit with their feet on the handlebars, legs crossed, backward, one foot, no hands—showtime.

Shots ring out, *buck! buck! buck!* The crowd stampedes like the running of the bulls. Girls scream. This way, that way, everybody zigzagging. Police horses screech, kick high, and charge the crowd. I catch Amir's eyes—heavy, alert, and breathing like glowing coals. I lose him and Scoop in the chaos. I scan the faces, but they're gone. More shots pop in the night. I run with the flow of the crowd to avoid getting trampled. I push up against the backs of strangers, dominoing around, drifting farther and farther into darkness.

I walk home alone, thinking about the last time I saw Amir.

24

Homegoing

In Loving Memory of Our Beloved . . .

* * * *

AMIR SMITH

June 21, 1982–July 13, 1998

Thursday, July 16, 1998

Wake: 8:30 p.m. Funeral: 9:00 p.m.

In the Sanctuary of New Refuge

1101-A N. Division Street

Philadelphia, PA

OBITUARY

Suddenly, in a senseless act of violence, Amir Jackson was called home. He was born June 21, 1982, in Philadelphia, PA, to Carleen Jackson. He attended various schools in the public school system. He leaves to hold on to his memory mother Carlee Smith and countless friends.

ORDER OF SERVICE

Opening Hymn—"Blessed Assurance"

* * * *

Prayer—Elder Dukes

* * * *

Scripture—Psalm 23:4

* * * *

"Yea, though I walk through the valley of the shadow of death, I will fear no evil: for thou art with me; thy rod and thy staff they comfort me."

Scripture—John 14:27

* * * *

"Peace I leave with you, my peace I give unto you: not as the world giveth, give I unto you. Let not your heart be troubled, neither let it be afraid."

Acknowledgment of Condolences

* * * *

Eulogy

* * * *

I don't know what happened that night, but things happen for a reason. I don't know why it happened to you, Amir. I've been looking for you to come in the house and say, "Where is that old woman?" Fear not, my dear son, your pain was only temporary. You are now one of God's soldiers. I will always love you.

—MOMMY

I keep asking myself why it had to be you. It seems like a nightmare. I feel I can't go on, but I know I must. Remember what Mom always said: "Go look for a job because the job won't come to you." So when I get a job, I'll tell Mom we have one. I'll be working and you'll be looking down to make sure I go all the way, making the big bucks. I'll miss you and I love you.

—YOUR SISTER, DENA

I love you and will never forget the things you taught me. 1LOVE.

—YOUR BROTHER, MALO

25

Killadelphia, Pistolvania

A gleaming black casket lined with satin cream ruffles. The smells of talcum powder, oil sheen, and death float through the tight room.

Tears explode from dark sockets, streak across puffy brown cheeks, and run under veils.

"When are y'all going to wake up?" the funeral director asks us. "Y'all got to wake up now . . . or rest in peace." After the service he calls all the young people to the back of the funeral home.

Ryan leans over to me. "I don't even care who, Malo, but somebody got to pay." He tells me to keep my suit on. "Or whatever you might want to get buried in." He's got two gats on him like *Face/Off*.

"While revenge weakens society, forgiveness gives it strength," the director says.

I'm numb to the world. A chunk of my soul is gone, and even offing the ngh that did it—if we knew who did it—

wouldn't bring my best friend back. I hear his funny voice—*Malo, you so black you showed up to my funeral naked*—but a cold, pained grimace is as close as I get to laughter. I know his playful self would want me to laugh, to smile, but I can't. Amir's mom sobs with a veil over her face, eyes as thin as paper cuts. I pull out the chain Amir left at my house the other day, the one he always wore, hand it to her.

She gives it back. "He wanted you to have it," she whispers under soft piano sounds. I put it on and tell myself I'll never take it off.

Long barrel automatics released in short bursts
The length of black life is treated with short worth*

"I know y'all are hurting, I'm hurting too. Every week I'm burying kids. Babies in boxes. Younger and younger each year: twelve, thirteen, fourteen, fifteen. Virgins! A young person dies and us old folks imagine all of the experiences we would have wished for you . . . You aren't even giving yourselves a chance at life, a chance to be lawyers, doctors, teachers. You're giving it all up to be statistics!"

He shows us the coffins and tells us, "The little ones, for teenagers like y'all, are my best sellers and business is booming! Booming! . . . But I want you to put me out of business. Put me under! I'd rather sink than to have to keep burying babies."

I think about how we used to brag about Philly being the murder capital—*da murda cappy*—and how this year, in Philly, we

* "Thieves in the Night," Black Star, 1998.

got more dead bodies than days. Shit ain't cool. Anybody can get it. Amir wasn't even the target. Nghz can't even aim 'cause they got no direction.

Some kid behind me says, "I can't die yet anyway, ain't got nobody to pay for my funeral."

Me and Ryan spark a blunt and hotbox the car on our way home. Smoke curls through the whip as we drive through the city, buzzing by faces. I study each one. The cops don't have a suspect, so everyone we drive past, pull up next to, or see on the street is a possible suspect. The cops are suspect for not having any suspects. They never have any suspects when we die. Tupac gets shot, dies, no suspects. Biggie gets shot, dies, no suspects. Big L gets shot, dies, no suspects. Amir gets shot, dies, no suspects. My soul weeps for Amir, for all the Amirs in this city.

We blaze until our eyes bleed.

26

The Pipeline

We pour into Fels High like syrup, steady and slow.

This school looks just like jail. I wonder why mad schools look like jails. Or do jails look like schools? The jail Uzi's in actually looks nicer than this. If schools look like prisons, and prisons look like schools, will we act like students or prisoners? Police roam the hallways whirling nightsticks like band directors. The windows are tinted with bars. No sunlight like a casino and you never win in here either.

At my old school, Friends, the teachers always fucked with me. At Fels, the teachers don't know who the fuck I am. Overcrowded like Amistad. Fels is the opposite of my old school, Friends—Foes. They say Foes is one of the best schools in the city. They say Fels is one of the worst. Foes, private. Fels, pub. Foes, mostly white. Fels, mostly black. Foes kids' parents got tuition money. Fels kids' parents ain't even got lunch money.

—

The metal detector line is long like the line to get into Club Dancers on Saturday nights. A bucket full of lighters, nail files, pocket knives. Everybody beeping, police digging through bags like moles. It takes forever to get in.

The hallway is a fashion show. Muhfuckas won't even come to school if they ain't got something fresh to throw on.

The bell goes off like we're in some factory somewhere. Here.

First period—

I think this is homeroom. The teacher never shows up so no one really knows. Girls just sit and do their makeup and hair. I dip in and out of the pissy hallways.

"Take your hat off . . . Pull up your pants . . . Where's your hall pass?" The guards yell every fifteen seconds like a recording. I act like I'm going to take my fitted off, then pull it down. I pull my pants up and let them fall back down—kiss my ass, toy cops.

I spill Remy on imaginary graves
Put my hat on my waves*

The pyros light the trash cans on fire around this time. The smoke detectors don't work, so the bathrooms are on Amsterdam, smoke clouds thick enough to hold rain. The first fight always jumps off around this time, either in class or in the hallway. We chase the fights like Action News reporters run

* "Take It in Blood," Nas, 1996.

after stories. Motherfuckers get their ass beat coming into school in the morning and leaving in the afternoon.

Sometimes this Chinese teacher, Mr. Lee, comes in and takes roll.

"Yo," this kid Lamont says real loud after Mr. Lee calls my name on the first day of school. The whole class turns to hear what he's about to say. "What the fuck is a Malo?" Everybody laughs. Lamont is strong but he's slower than a tar drip, too slow to see it coming. I show him what a Malo is, right there in the middle of the class, hit him with the punch my uncle Jabbar showed me, make him swallow and spit at the same damn time.

Second period—

"Turn off your beepers and cell phones" is how Ms. Mackey greets us every morning. Nobody turns shit off. My jawn vibrates like an engine on my hip. I don't even know what class this is or what Mackey teaches. The flickering fluorescence over our heads reminds me of hospitals and nightmares. There's never enough seats, so if you don't snag one early, she makes you stand up against the wall like a wallflower at a house party. This one day, when there are no seats, she gives me the evil eye 'cause I sit on the desk.

"Whatever your name is—off the desk!" she barks. She doesn't know anybody's name. When she calls roll, she just listens, never even looks up.

"My leg hurts," I say, all in my I-shall-not-be-moved Rosa Parks bag.

"Off the damn desk!"

"Don't talk to him like that." My homegirl Tamara jumps

up. "You need to get some more seats up in here." Tamara is always rumble ready. Sometimes she comes to school in her fight gear: sweatpants, beat-up Reebok Classics, fake Gucci scarf, Vaseline face.

Mackey grabs the phone and, within seconds, police with crooked mugs and big black boots are dragging us out. Her class is stupid anyway, you just copy whatever she writes on the board, which doesn't usually make sense. If someone asks a question, she calls them "ulcers" and starts talking about how she doesn't even want to be here and how she gets paid either way. Sometimes she's too lazy to come and we get a sub—fresh meat.

Every period I think about Amir. Sometimes it feels like he's right there, sitting next to me cracking jokes and sunflower seeds.

Third, fourth, and fifth periods—

Lunch, lunch, and lunch. Every student is assigned a lunch, either third, fourth, or fifth period. I don't know which lunch I am . . . so I always hit up all three. The cafeteria guard doesn't say shit because he's a customer, buys an eighth of Sour Diesel from me every other week.

The cafeteria: bananas, pure chaos. The benches and tables are bolted down and midget-low from when this used to be a middle school. There's always a couple fights during the first lunch, mostly girls, haymakers and windmills, boobs popping out like Jell-O, spinning, spitting, a lot of hair pulling. The fights leave weave tracks and braids scattered on the floor, right there with the spilled milk, baked beans, and textbooks facing down, pages open like dead birds.

—

Fourth lunch is live because that's when my homies Q-Demented, QD, this Puerto Rican rap crew from Olney, come through and murder the cypher. They roll into lunch mad deep like Wu Tang. It's usually Apathy, Blacastan, Block McCloud, Celph Titled, Crypt the Warchild, Demoz, Des Devious, Doap Nixon, Esoteric, Journalist, Jus Allah, King Magnetic, King Syze, Planetary, Reef the Lost Cauze, Vinnie Paz, and V-Zilla. I huddle with them and kick freestyles:

King Syze

In Philly don't let nothing but the Uzi spray
My only concern really, is who got paid

QD

One by one you all fall in this game
Comin with the wild out style you can't tame
QD no matter where we going all, we all for it
Don't step in the path when the plan's in full orbit

Jedi

Illadelph is like the sun 'cause we shine with rhymes
Underground is like the moon, you only see us at times

Planetary

Out for the green, I'll make you scream
Like chicks gettin tag-teamed in porno scenes

Jus Allah

I like to fight with the hammer, south side of the camera sight,
And I stand by my words like Vanna White

Boom box, beat box, or table drum, don't matter—the beat goes on like life does. Girls come around, dance, back it up for us real quick, and stomp away laughing.

Fifth lunch is the Wild West.

I shoot dice with the get-money boys in the corner. I shake, roll, then jump back fast like bacon's popping.

"Door blow . . . head crack . . . faded . . . bet, bet, bet . . ." as red dice tumble around fresh Timbs, Air Maxes, and Jordans. Sometimes I come up a couple hunnit, sometimes not. That's the game, like life, mountains and valleys, ups and downs.

Fifth lunch is like a slaughterhouse, the killing fields. Gang fights, knives, all-out food fights, even race wars: Cambos vs. blacks, Puerto Rocks vs. blacks, whites vs. everybody. Me, I'm cool with all the races. My favorite color is green.

—

I don't know what classes I have after fifth period; I never stay longer than the last lunch. There's really no point. There's no learning going on at Fels, just rules and yelling and chaos and screaming correctional-officer teachers. I feel like I can learn more outside of these dead school walls.

Every day I dip out the back door of the cafeteria, hop the metal fence, and speed away from the school that looks like jail, feels like jail. They do what they always do, the only thing they know how to do, what jails do: punish me with detention and probation, like the judge did Uzi.

27

Shape-Up

—"'Sup, this Malo. Right place, wrong time. You know the drill . . ."

—*10

—"Welcome. You have eleven new messages . . ."

In Fresh Cutz barbershop getting my weekly shape-up, checking the voice mail on my new Motorola StarTAC. I give everybody my new number, even my school so they don't stress my mom with their BS. I keep my hair in a low, dark hustla jawn with long sideburns. In Philly, a fresh cut is mandatory. Jawns be like, *Damn, ngh, you wolfin,* if your shit ain't sharp.

—"What's up, Malo? Dis Keisha from the other night, at Gotham. Hit me up, boo." *Message deleted.*

—"Son, it's your father. I'm trying to connect with you. How are you? Call me back, please. I want to see you, need to see you, it's been way too long." *Message deleted.*

Fresh Cutz is around my old way in Olney. They sell

everything: DVDs, water ice, birthday cards, socks, incense, whatever. They're always selling random shit. When I walk in, Mike, my barber, asks me, "You know anyone who wants to buy some vending machines?" Mike is a cool old head hustleman. He's pigeon-toed, which makes all his sneaks lean.

"Vending machines?" I laugh. "Nah."

—"This is a very important automated message from the School District of Philadelphia; please listen carefully . . . Hello, this is Samuel Fels High School calling about your child's attendance who was absent today, missing all scheduled periods. Please call the office—" *Message deleted*.

The crackheads outside the shop are wiping down my new whip: a baby-blue Ford Explorer coupe, eighteen-inch Asanti wheels, 5 percent limo tint, an Xtant/JL Audio system so loud you can hear me coming from a block away.

"That muhfucka bad," the smokers say when I pull up. I can feel all the girls in the salon next to the shop checking for me when I pull up. Driving this car, hanging with Scoop, and getting paid has got grown-ass women throwing the panties at me. MILF jawns with mortgages and kids my age.

—"I don't even know why I would even believe that you would call me back after I let you hit. You're a trifling-ass person but it's cool 'cause karma's a bitch and I wish I could be there when it bites you in the ass! Fuck you, you stupid lying-ass bitch . . . Oh, and I'm not trying to make you feel some type of way because I'm sure you don't even give a fuck but—" *Message deleted*.

—"Son, it's your father. Please call me." *Message deleted*.

I'm blowing money faster than a hollow-tip. I get it, I spend it. It takes my mind off the bullshit: off the fact that my best friend is gone, my mom is in a coma, my dad left, my sister's on the funny farm, and my brother is locked in a dog kennel in Arizona. I run through Vizuris and Bloomingdale's and Neiman Marcus with Scoop. Versace. Iceberg. Moschino. Ralph Lauren Purple Label. Tommy Hill. YSL. Jordans. Timbs. Air Maxes. DKNY. Gucci. We walk out of the mall swinging bags like bandits.

My Moschino hoe, my Versace hottie
Come to find out you was fuckin everybody*

I'm like my mom in that way, I like all the finer things in life. Everything I want is expensive. It's crazy that people only say hello and thank you in this city when you're in a store buying shit. When you're spending money, everyone is your friend. People open doors, smile at you, laugh at your jokes, apologize all the time. *Let me get that for you . . . Can I help you? . . . May I? . . .* Fake fucks.

New Jack City is on in the barbershop. Nino's like: "I'm not guilty. You're the one that's guilty. The lawmakers, the politicians, the Colombian drug lords, all you who lobby against making drugs legal. Just like you did with alcohol during the prohibition. You're the one who's guilty. I mean, c'mon, let's kick the ballistics here: Ain't no Uzis made in Harlem. Not

* "Get Money," Junior M.A.F.I.A., 1996.

one of us in here owns a poppy field. This thing is bigger than Nino Brown. This is big business. This is the American way."

—"Stay away from my girl, dog, forreal. Keisha's mine. I'm not gon' tell you again, man, she mine." *Message deleted.*

I realize you can spend any amount of money too. The more you get, the more you spend. I used to think a thousand dollars was a lot of money, but me and Scoop blow that in a night now. My Versace jacket cost a G. No matter how much I spend, though, the pain is still there, it never goes away, like a tattoo.

—"Malo, it's Bone. Hit me up, let's get this paper." *Message deleted.*

I'm spending money and, at the same time, learning all types of interesting things about money. I don't even call it "paper" anymore like everybody else does because money isn't actually paper—it's cotton, the same cotton my dad picked, his dad, and his dad before that. One of my customers works at the Mint in Old City, he showed me how they make money. I broke him off with an eighth of Purple Haze and showed him how I make money.

—"You are the most ignorant person I have ever met in my life! Fuck you, Malo! You ain't shit and I hope your ugly black ass gets hit by a truck—" *Message deleted.*

I also stop calling money "dead presidents." Jay-Z's got that song "Dead Presidents" where he samples Nas on the hook, saying, "I'm out for presidents to represent me." Then there's that movie *Dead Presidents* with the chick blasting out of the dumpster in whiteface. But Benjamin Franklin is on the hundred-dollar bill and he wasn't a president. Then there's Alexander Hamilton on the ten-dollar bill, John Marshall on the five hundred, and Salmon P. Chase on the ten thousand, and none of them were presidents either.

I'm an addict for sneakers
20s of buddah and bitches with beepers*

—"A chick who knows her position will never lose her place . . . I know my position, so hit me up, boo . . . Ashley." *Message deleted.*

Mike is telling everybody why he thinks Tupac is still alive. "He's alive, man, he's alive, he's alive," he says like Frankenstein. "No pictures of him in the hospital . . . No funeral, no viewing . . . He changed his name to Machiavelli. That's the ngh that faked his death . . . In the video for 'I Ain't Mad At Cha' he's already in heaven, the shit was planned . . . His last album was called *The 7 Day Theory* and he was shot on September seventh, survived until the thirteenth—seven days!—then died . . . In 'Toss It Up' and 'To Live and Die in L.A.' he's rocking the Air Jordans and the Pennys that didn't come out until after he died . . . In 'God Bless the Dead' he says 'Rest in peace' to my ngh Biggie Smalls, but Pac was murdered before Biggie . . . Explain that!"

—"Son, this is your father. Why are you doing this? Why—" *Message deleted.*

"But you know how I really know Pac is alive? How I really, really know?"

"How you know?"

"'Cause real nghz don't die."

—"It's me . . . Nia." *Message saved.*

* "N.Y. State of Mind," Nas, 1994.

Dear Carole,

I get up when I can, I eat when I want to, I bathe when it is absolutely necessary, and I sleep even as I wake.

I no longer talk about suffering. Everyone suffers. It is about expectations. If your expectations aren't met, then you suffer in some way. The intensity of your suffering has to do with how invested you were in your expectations. Even those who give up and say they don't have any expectations have the expectation of no expectation, so they suffer as well. I didn't play the game of "my pain is greater than yours." Pain, after all, was pain. Was there something greater than pain?

I have about seven scars on my belly from various surgeries. They are my lifelines. Each time I went under the knife I wasn't certain that I would survive, and with each surgery I began to wonder if I should survive. My husband could not hide his wishes that I shouldn't survive. My belly is etched with my history and my life. Both of my sons have made their marks there and so I wear these marks with pride. They are symbols of a terrible beauty that speaks to life.

Malo is—

28

Burn

"What are you doing?" I slam the journal closed but it's too late—I'm caught. My mom studies her secret words between my palms. "Why are you reading my journal?" She's standing in the doorway to my room, eyes glassy from meds, staring at me like I broke her heart.

She snatches her journal from me. "How could you?" she asks, thumbing through the pages as if to make sure they're all there. "How could you violate me like that? How could you?"

When it rains, it pours. Her eyes fall on my table—on my gun, my pound of weed, and all my money. Her face tightens. She sees the piles of new clothes on my bed. She grabs as much gear as she can hold, then power walks out of my room. I follow her out to the terrace. She hurls my clothes over the railing.

I bolt downstairs.

". . . the fuck," seeing more shit flying down: It's a bird, it's a plane—no, it's fly gear falling from the sky like parachutes. It all settles on the concrete like autumn leaves over puddles.

I grab what I can grab and come upstairs dragging my clothes through the hallway. She's thrown some of my clothes in the hallway too. I try to open the door but the top lock stops me. I bang on the door like five-o.

"Ma?" *Bang-bang-bang.* I feel her on the other side of the door.

"What?" she says, cold.

"Open the door, Ma."

She's at the door like a bouncer. "No . . . I want you out of my house."

"Where I'm s'pose to go?"

"I don't care. You're old enough to sell drugs, carry a gun, steal my journal behind my back? Then you're old enough to be on your own."

"I was trying to help you."

"Help me? You're never here! You don't care about me." Her words feel like punches to the throat.

"I'm not the one that left you. Where your friends at? Huh? Where's Dad? Where's Uzi? I'm the only one still here!"

"Out!"

I can't believe this shit. "You kicking me out, Ma?"

"Yes, I want you out!" *Maybe the pills got her spazzing?* Someone gets off the elevator, sees the chaos, keeps it moving.

Me and my mom just stand there for a minute, different sides of the tracks, listening to each other's breath. Hers is heavy and distant like a freight train.

"Alright, Ma, I'll leave . . . but open the door first, I gotta get my stuff." I'm not scared. I have enough money and bud to get my own spot, to make moves on my own. I don't need nobody. Fuck it.

I get on my linebacker shit and hit the door with my shoulder like it's a running back coming through the middle. Pops open. I slide past her and go to my room.

All of my shit—the weed, money, gun—is gone, everything gone.

"Where is it?" The table is a blank page.

"Out!" she screams after me.

"Where's my shit, Ma?" I'm looking around the room, searching, panicking.

"I threw it away." I run to the trash. Dig through. Nothing.

"Where's it at, Ma? I ain't playin."

"The incinerator."

"You're toxic," I say, looking right at her. She smacks the dog shit out of me. My face on fire.

My last words: "Now I see why Dad left."

29

Spaceships and Crowns

A nation of questions: *Where to stay? Who to stay with? Who to call? Where the fuck am I going? Where to get money? What am I going to do about Bone's money? What's the point . . . of life? Who killed Amir? Who am I? Am I who I say I am? Why am I here, in Philly, in America, on Earth, right now? What's my purpose?*

I hit 10 Gs, thinking, *I'll crash at Ted's crib, lay low, and plot my next move*. I spot the crew, standing where they always stand, between the liquor store and the corner store, next to the Fern Rock Apartments fence, under the train tracks, and across the street from Rock Steady, this bugged ngh who sits on a crate all day with a broken radio, rocking his head back and forth to a beat no one else can hear.

Everything looks the same, except them. They're all rocking baby Afros and wearing all black everything, like Darth Vader. I feel like I missed a memo.

"Peace, brother Malo." I laugh, thinking, *Brother Malo? How long have I been gone?* Since I moved to G-Town, I haven't been around here much. Plus I don't understand why none of them came to Amir's funeral.

"What's up with the 'fros?"

Ted pulls out a long pick with a black fist on the handle, fluffs his 'fro. "Crowns," he says.

"What?"

"These are our crowns," cuffing it. "In the Bible, Samson got his power from his hair." He looks at my fresh cut. "Malo, you keep going to the barbershop, losing your power, losing your crown."

" 'Thou shalt not mar the corner of thy beard.' Leviticus 19:27," D-Rock reads from a book with a glowing black man drawn on the cover.

"Let me hit that," I say, reaching for the strange little blunt Ted is blazing. He doesn't pass it.

"It's a beedi . . . not weed."

"It get you high?" I ask. "I'm stressed."

"No high, just sacred Indian herbs."

I ask them for a forty and they say it's liquid crack.

"Take a chicken bone, the wishbone, and drop it in a bottle of malt liquor—OE, Steel Reserve, St. Ides, Crazy Horse, Hurricane, Midnight Dragon, Colt 45—that shit will dissolve in under a minute. It's poison, brother."

Huh? But these are the nghz that slid me my first forty, made me take my first shot of Henny, passed me my first blunt, handed me my first gun. I step away from 10 Gs for a couple of months and they turn square?

"Da fuck is going on with y'all? The 'fros, the gear, poison?" I say.

They call it Right Knowledge.

D-Rock's like, "There's nothing left, so we gotta be right. Right Knowledge leads to right thinking, and right thinking leads to right action. We are a part of the Holy Tabernacle Ministries . . . the Egyptian Church of Karast . . . the Holy Seed Baptist Synagogue . . . the Ancient Order of Melchizedek . . . the Ancient Order . . . the United Nuwaubian Nation of Moors . . . Yamasse Native American Tribe . . . the Washitaw Tribe."

"Real eyes realize real lies," Ted says, gazing into my eyes. It's like he's in a trance, like he's under a spell. I hear the *Twilight Zone* theme.

"Yo, y'all in a cult?" I can't believe this. Uzi's not going to believe this shit.

"The Holy Tabernacle Ministries is no cult. Check yourself, man."

They call the leader Dr. York. They talk about him like God and say something about how they're going down to Georgia to live in some pyramid he built.

"He has seventy trillion years of knowledge."

"What's his name?"

"Dr. Malachai Z. York . . . Imperial Grand Potentate

Noble: Rev. Dr. York 33 Degrees/720 Degrees . . . Malachi Zodok . . . Amunubi Rah Ka Ptah . . . Abba Issa . . . the One . . . Isa Abd'Allah Ibn Abu Bakr Muhammad . . . Akhtah Isa Jabbarlah . . . the Angel Michael . . . Murdoq . . . El Qubt . . . the Green One . . . Yanuwn . . . Rabboni Y'shua Bar El Haady . . . Sabathil . . . Maku . . . Baba Bassa Afrika . . . the Master Teacher . . . the Grand Hierophant . . . Chief Black Thunderbird Eagle . . . the Reformer."

They pop in a CD:

". . . Where are you going? Where we came from. Where have we come from? Every place and no place, so come, let's go . . . I am a being from the nineteenth galaxy called Illyuwn. We have been coming to this planet before it had your life-form on it. I manifest into this body to speak through this body. I am a entity, an etheric being . . ."

"Y'all serious?"

"Dead serious."

". . . My incarnation as an Ilah Mutajassid or avatar was originally in the year 1945 A.D. In order to get here I traveled by one of the smaller passenger crafts called SHAM out of a mother plane called Nibiru. I am an Anunnaqi or what you would call an Extraterrestrial; I am what you call an Angelic being, an Eloheem from the eighth planet Rizq . . . I have incarnated here in this form for the sole purpose of saving the children of the Eloheem, the Nubians, the chosen 144,000 . . ."

They ask me what I think about all this.

I think of this Richard Pryor flick Uzi used to watch all the time. Richard Pryor is sitting down, making crazy faces, smoking. Goes: "In my neighborhood, you know, there used to be some beautiful black men that would come through the neighborhood, dressed in African shit, you know. Really, now, you know, 'Peace and love, remember the essence of life, we are people of the universe, life is beautiful.' My parents would go, 'That ngh is crazy.' I used to love to go to the meetings, though, when you get down. I got ultra black for a while. Brothers would be rappin, I never knew what they were saying, though. But the brothers would be having them motions. 'You see the first thing you got to know is about eating pork. Now you eat a piece of pork, you don't realize the suffocations of this individuality's prospect. What the man is trying to lay on you through porkitis, you would not understand, because the trichinosis of your mind would not relinquish the thought of individuality. You know what I mean?' Now that ngh is crazy."

I'm standing here, listening to spaceships and stars, and all I can think is: *These nghz are crazy . . . even crazier than the Hebrew Israelites with the bullhorns and Afrika Bambaata outfits at Broad and Olney.*

I also think it's kind of cool, though. Cool that they're into something, something besides the block. They're teaching themselves, questioning stuff, and trying to figure this crazy world out—and that's dope.

They give me a copy of a book called *Behold a Pale Horse*. The cover has white horses, black horses, fires, angels, chariots, the devil, and heaven and hell on it. Shit looks like a nightmare. They tell me that politics is politicks because ticks are bloodsuckers. Human is hue man. American is Ameri-con. Nubian is new being. They call me an A-alike.

"A-alike 'cause we B-alike and C-alike."

They say they are part of the chosen—the 144,000 Eloheems that are going to board the mother ship.

"When?" I ask.

"Y2K. The year 2000. That's when we board Nibiru and leave this galaxy."

"Let me see your hand, Malo." I put it out like I'm trying on a ring. He studies my hand.

"Look," he says to D-Rock. D-Rock looks at my hand.

"Fuck y'all doin?"

"Making sure you ain't no reptilian. Reptilians are disagreeable beings, opposed to the existence of humanity. You can tell by their fingers, if they got webs or not. And they got grayish skin 'cause they evolved from dinosaurs. Their hair grows in sixes, like white people's, hence six-six-six. Our hair, the Eloheems', the black man's hair, grows in nines."

A cult, though? A cult? Uzi won't believe me if I tell him. I'm learning to expect the unexpected.

I don't even ask Ted if I can crash at his spot. He's acting too weird. I just pull off while they go on ramming about crowns and spaceships. I chuck the deuces and keep it moving.

Alone in the streets.

30

No Place to Be Somebody

No place to be somebody. I can go everywhere but can stay nowhere. I feel like the blunt I'm smoking, burning way too fast. Sixteen going on what? I dip from spot to spot, going through chambers like a Shaolin warrior lost on an impossible quest.

I go to Bone's house to work something out. I owe him three Gs because the pound my mom burned up was given to me on consignment. I didn't pay for it yet.

In his dark, dirty basement, with his pit bulls barking non-stop and his goons palming pistols on the couch, he tells me cold: "I'll give you until the end of the week. That's it."

I think about what Amir told me about Damien—how he killed someone over a hundred bucks, off principle—and how I only really know Bone and Damien through Amir, and how Amir wasn't even that cool with them. I feel dead already.

—

I drive around the city thinking of my next move.

I miss everybody: Amir, Mom, Dad, Uzi. I think about them all as I cruise through South Phil, blunted, eyes low, plotting my next move. I wonder if Amir can see me now, can picture me rollin. I wonder if Uzi can see me. He doesn't call, write, nothing.

Uzi it hurts, leave you double-dead
I'm a bubble-head
I never listened to nothing my mother said*

I keep falling asleep behind the wheel. I just wake up . . . driving . . . and I'm like, *Damn, how long was I asleep for?* It's usually for a few seconds, but still. I dream quick dreams like flashes of broken light. A flash of Zimbabwe, of Uzi, Mom, Dad, happier days.

I think it's because most nights I don't sleep. I stay up all night, up with the night workers and nightwalkers, dope fiends and crooked cops, the stars and the nghz under them searching for stripes, pimps and stick-up kids, truck drivers and dope boys, take-out spots and road crews, hoodies and heels, dungeons and dragons. I love the night. Everything, everyone, everywhere changes when the sun dips.

I never *go* to sleep. I might crash, pass out, fall out, dip, but I never *go*. I'm like a ngh on the run and sleep is the cops, trying

* "Banned from TV," Big Pun (Capone-N-Noreaga featuring Nature, Big Pun, Cam'ron, Styles P, and Jadakiss), 1998.

to take me off the streets, slow me down. I might get locked up, but I ain't turning myself in. I don't *go* to sleep.

I wake up everywhere, different parts of the city, usually still high and drunk from the night before, usually on the floor. You can't fall out of bed when you sleep on the floor . . . or in the car.

—S—

I wake up on Marshall Street in South Philly. I stay in Kam's basement with him and his cousin J-Money. It's a cave that smells like pussy, cologne, and crack. Kam's mom goes to work and Kam goes to school—I haven't been in months—so me and J-Money chill on the block during the day. He's like nineteen, sells crack, and gets off on fuckin other nghz' girls. That's his thing, always talking about "Don't bring your girl around me, dog."

Bone keeps hitting my cell, but I don't answer. He wants his money and I don't have it, so there's nothing to talk about.

Fiends always at the window on Marshall Street, yellow fingernails like *tap tap tap*. The crack is stashed outside, everywhere: in crumpled Checkers and Wendy's bags in the trash; inside tennis balls; behind a brick in the wall; in a dirty mattress in the alley. One day he's taking a dump and asks me to make the sale. Fuck it. I go out there and it's J-Money's grandma, standing there, fidgeting like a first-grader. She hands me the dirtiest ten-dollar bill I've ever seen. I drop it and run back into the basement.

"Yo, it's your grandma," I say outside the bathroom door.

"Serve her!" he says, toilet flushing. I don't. He does.

Cuz being a ngh means you love nghz
So how could you love nghz if you tryna drug nghz?*

I bounce the next day, tripping on how the streets turn you cold, how money has us out here like zombies, killing each other for crumbs.

—W—

I wake up on Frazier Street in West Philly.

Staying here with Amir's cousin June. The house is across the street from a church with a lawn sign that says *God Saves.* I think, *Bullshit. Saves who? Not Amir. Saves what? When? Whatever.*

The block is quiet during the day. These old heads play chess on the hood of an old Chevy Monte Carlo. They call me over one day, try to read me, see what I'm about. One of them, he's got his cane resting on his knee, tells me I'm not a man yet.

"You ain't a man until you learn that your dick is either a commodity, a tool, or a weapon."

"My dick is just big," I laugh, and go back in the house.

One day they tell me some guys came around looking for me.

"Asked if we knew where you were."

"You sure?"

"They said your name. Malo. About three or four of 'em. Ugly fellas too. I hope you ain't in no trouble."

I rack my brain. No one knows I'm here except June. It's

* "N.I.G.G.A. (Never Ignorant Getting Goals Accomplished)," 2Pac, 1998.

got to be Bone and Damien trying to collect. I leave that night, keep it moving.

I learn to always keep it moving, never stay anywhere too long. They say if you drop a frog in boiling water, it'll jump out. But if you drop it in room-temp water and slowly heat it up, the frog sits there and dies. I'm trying to be the frog that gets the jump on the boil. So I'm learning to see as far as possible and, same time, avoid being seen, lay in the cut like peroxide. I'm growing eyes that hear and ears that see. The only ones who make it out here are the nghz that move fast. So I keep my train moving so I don't get moved on. Harder to hit a moving target.

I drive around the city looking at the shapes the shadows make on the ground, against the buildings, on people. Philly is a city of shapes. Out here everybody has an angle, like geometry. Squares trying to box me in. Octagons trying to stop me. Circles trying to throw me for a loop. Everything on the line. The sooner I catch the angle, the better off I am.

—N—

I wake up on Allegheny Ave., staying with Scoop. Kianna told me to stay away from him but this is a last resort. I don't even know who lives in this house. It's just a spot full of random people coming and going—turnstile. It's above a Korean corner store, so we chill in front of there a lot. I wonder why—wonder when, wonder how—Koreans who don't speak much English just come up in the hood, set up shop, and make mad bank off nghz. Fuck it—it is what it is—I ain't mad at 'em. Everybody gotta eat.

Normal corner store shit: quarter hug juice, chips, blunts, beer, cigs, and straight-shooter crack pipes right next to the candy. Scoop's always arguing with them.

"A pack of Pall Malls."

"Pall Malls?" I say. Every black person I've ever met smokes Newports.

"I like designer clothes, Versace, Moschino, Polo, but I'm not paying for no designer name-brand cancer. Give me the cheap shit."

When Scoop was with Kianna, everybody knew he had screws loose, but now that they're apart, it's clear that his screws are actually gone for good. Kianna's the only one who can calm him down. Every day he's beefing with nghz, robbing people, fighting, and creating enemies. One night the house gets lit up. A drive-by. I'm sleeping on the floor when it happens. Glass exploding. People screaming. Tires screeching. I leave the same night.

—E—

I wake up in my car under a bridge in Logan. Alone with my heartbeat. Get out to pee.

"Run that shit!" I'm got. This hairy-face ngh, gat in palm, eyes like tinted windows with air bubbles. The other boy, corn bread husky, grim-reaper hoodie on, looks out.

"Hurry up." He pats my pockets. "Run all that shit!" He helps me take it off. Snatches my beeper. Spots the chain, the one Amir gave me, under my rugby. "Chain too," he orders like it's already his. And that's the last straw. It hits me—I don't even care if I die, fuck it, I ain't got shit to live for. I'm ready to die for this chain Amir loved so much, his prized possession and the only thing his pops left him.

"Shoot!"

"Bang 'im."

He rips the chain from me.

"You Muslim?" He stops struggling with me, studying the chain. Seems like everybody in Philly is Muslim. I nod fast. He looks at his friend—they talk to each other without speaking. He pushes the chain into my fist, then gives me all my shit back.

"My bad . . . Salamu alaikum," he says, and fades into the night.

Amir's chain is broken but I'm just relieved that I still have it.

I find out later the charm says *Allah,* which means "God" in Arabic.

I remember the sign on Frazier Street: *God Saves.*

31

On the Road

Ryan shows up in the middle of the night, sweating, heaving, eyes breathing like glowing coals, the way Amir's looked the last time I saw him. We just leave—before he even tells me the whole story about how he's on the run, what went down—we just hit the highway and don't look back.

"They coming for me, Malo," he says as I chug down I-95, windows down, music blasting. I feel like they're coming for me too: the cops, Bone, Damien, Scoop's enemies.

"Slow down, Malo, they got a APB out."

"APB?"

"All points bulletin."

We pull over at a rest stop, fill the tank, and spend our last few bucks on snacks and a map of America. We spread the country out on the dash of my Explorer. We're in Delaware.

"Where you wanna go?"

"Anywhere. Just away from here."

Embrace the wheel and hit a buck without crashin fuck
My drug passion got a nigga stashin fast what*

I call my older cousin Chris, who lives in Ft. Worth, Texas. "Y'all fools need to come down here to the Funky . . . tell 'em he can stay down here and lay low." Chris came to stay with us in Philly a few years ago and remembers Ryan. He's cool as shit, from L.A., straight outta Compton like N.W.A. "Bompton" is how he reps it. He claims Ft. Worth too. He stays with us for like a year, goes to community college, and puts me on to Texas hip-hop: Geto Boys, UGK, Rap-a-Lot Records, DJ Screw.

"Say no more," he tells me on the phone. "Come on, kinfolk! What y'all waitin on?"

We drive through Richmond and Raleigh, through Memphis and Little Rock. We watch the sun rise, set, and then rise again, like watching reruns of a miracle. I bask in the miracle, in the warmth of its rays, in its rise, fall, and redemption.

Nighttime comes and swallows everything. Eighteen-wheelers roaring past like trains, then disappearing into the black.

In front of us, the horizon trembles in haze. Ryan drives. I pull out Noreaga's CD and, bored, peep the liner notes: *To my real thugs on da run eating—avoid court, da C.O.'s, da P.O.'s, county and state police. When in and out of state remember your name or attribute change with da town, so as u travel*

* "Channel 10," Capone-N-Noreaga, 1997.

remain eatin'. All authorities are crazy for trying to take on our destiny in their hands.

I think about Uzi, think about all the Uzis, all the Amirs, the Ryan, the Malos, running . . . from what? I don't know why I'm running but I feel like I can't stop. I'm tired but don't want to stop. Not the car, not the music, nothing. There's something scary about stopping, like in that movie *Speed,* where the bus has to go faster than fifty-five mph or else it blows up.

To stop: to die.

The only thing I know about Ft. Worth is that it's always the featured location on my mom's favorite show, *Cops* . . . and that my favorite cousin, Chris, is waiting for us to show up in Funkytown.

The air is hot and sticky like we're inside a plastic bag. Chris lives in an apartment complex and pushes a black Mustang.

"Y'all lil' nghz grab a beer and come on back," Chris says. He's got broad shoulders and dark curly hair. Hazel eyes that match his complexion. He's in his classic black hat—no logo, no team, just black with a bent brim.

We're at Chris' boys' crib. They play dominoes and yell shit like "Study long, study wrong . . . Fish wata stank . . . Follow that cab—it got dope in it . . . Getcha kids out the street . . . Domino motherfucker!"

These twins, Lil' Brain Dead and Half Gone, show up with this girl.

"Give the lil' nghz some head," one of them tells her.

"Okay, daddy," she says. "But one at a time . . . baby face first," pointing at me, strutting into the back room.

"Handle that." Chris hands me a Trojan. "Strap up." I go in first. She's laying on the bed playing with herself. I can't. I walk out of the room and it's a revolving door for the next couple of hours. Tag team. Choo-choo.

Let it sit inside your head like a million women in Philly, Penn.
It's silly when girls sell their soul because it's in*

All I can think about is Nia, my heart. She has the energy that holds this whole damn world together, that makes the sun rise. Her voice whispers to me thousands of miles away.

I call but it just keeps ringing . . .

My uncle Howard picks me up from Chris' in the morning. Gives me a giant bear hug. Tightest embrace ever. He has a slow, proud walk. Chest out.

"I'm eighty-one," he tells me. He can pass for fifty.

His house is an oasis. Like calm in the middle of a storm. We sit on the couch with my aunt Georgia and watch this movie *Powder,* about an albino boy with special powers. I check out the box cover, it reads, "An Extraordinary Encounter with Another Human Being."

We're all really feeling this movie. It feels like Powder is talking directly to me. He's like: *When a thunderstorm comes up, I can feel it inside. When lightning comes down, I can feel*

* "Doo Wop (That Thing)," Lauryn Hill, 1998.

it wanting to come to me. Grandma said it was God. She said the white fire was God . . . Energy, always relaying, always transforming, and never-ending . . . Have you ever listened to people from the inside? Listened so close you can hear their thoughts—and all their memories. Hear them think from places they don't even know they think from.

Me and my uncle talk about death, life, belief. He's a mystical man, a thinking man, with the widest, most inviting smile I've ever seen, ever felt.

"Walk with me." He leads the way in slow, proud strides. Big freckles like stars.

"I know about your friend," he says. *Know what?* I think. *That he's on the run? About the gun? The stash?* "I can tell by your eyes, you got something you want to say . . . but can't. Not yet." Crazy how he knows all this. I feel like he knows everything. About me, about Ryan, all the shit we're into. But he's not judging. Those eyes, deep like canyons, seeing right into my soul, doing something to me.

"I know."

We walk along a creek behind his house.

" 'Like black pearls trapped in the white cerebellum, we glisten out of reach of drum gun and talking bird . . . I want you to leap high in the sky with me until we see yellow trees and blue gulf.' "

I don't know what he's talking about. It's like he's speaking a foreign language, a foreign language I want to learn.

"Henry Dumas," he says. "Heard of him?"

I shake my head.

"Heads up," he says, pulling a thin book from his back

pocket and tossing it to me. I look at the cover: *Poetry for My People*.

"Check it out," he says. "Dumas was from my hometown. Sweet Home, Arkansas."

I stand at the edge of the water, on the edge of being, reflecting—on my mom and how I want to tell her, to show her, that I'm sorry; on Bone and how I'm going to stop running and face him like a man when I get back to Philly; about Uzi and how I don't want to end up in jail like him; about my dad and how I miss him; about what Amir said about fathers.

"'Let the beauty of what you love be what you do.'" He pats me on the shoulder. "That's Rumi."

Later on, at dinner, Uncle Howard tells me about the war inside.

"There's a war between two wolves inside everybody. One is anger, jealousy, greed, resentment, inferiority, lies, and ego. The other's good. It's love, peace, beauty, happiness, truth, hope, joy, humility, kindness, and empathy."

I'm thrust back to reality when my cousin Kianna hits me up. She's frantic. Out of breath. Tells me my mom OD'd . . . that they don't know if she's going to make it.

"Where are you?" she asks.

Me and Ryan at the doorway with our bags.

"I'll take my chances back up there . . . can't see myself living down here," Ryan tells me. He's coming back to Philly with me, facing the risk. "Is what it is."

I give long, deep hugs to Uncle Howard and Aunt Georgia,

then hop in the car with Ryan. I start the engine, then jump out, forgetting something.

I walk up to my uncle. "In the story," I ask, "who wins . . . between the two wolves?"

"The one you feed."

32

The White Fire

"Slow down, Malo." I hear Ryan, but my foot is heavy. Heart heavier. Speeding through Little Rock with the windows halfway down, feeling halfway between everywhere, right and wrong, past and present, life and death, me and me.

Between the no longer and the not yet.

Thunder, lightning, dark clouds swirling above us like vultures. We're driving straight through a storm from the Bible.

I think about the wolves inside me, growling, fighting.

Lightning in front of us, treetops flashing. We head right for it like an electric finish line in the sky.

No music, just storm.

White fire in the sky.

"Slow down, Malo." But I'm in go mode. I feel like scum for what I said to my mom. *If she dies, I don't deserve to live.*

I drive so fast, so hard, I don't even notice the cops on our ass. Ryan's jaw tightens in thought.

—

Speak when spoken to, say less than necessary, I tell myself as the trooper crushes gravel on his march toward us.

"What state we in?" Ryan asks me.

"I don't know, maybe Virginia."

"I tailed you for two miles at ninety mph." Pale stone face.

"My mom's in the hospital . . . I'm rushing to see her . . . Sorry, officer, I didn't realize how fast I was going."

"You said your mom's in the hospital?"

"Yes."

"So that gives you the right to speed through my county?"

"But she—"

"I could care less, boy," he says, scoping my system in the back: speakers, amp, neon bars. "Now look here: the only person with blue lights around here is going to be the law."

Cops like him are the reason for these songs: "Black and Blue" by Brand Nubian, "Coffee, Donuts and Death" by Paris, "Crooked Cops" by E-40, "Crooked Officer" by Geto Boys, "Dirty Cop Named Harry" by Hard Knocks, "Duck da Boyz" by Strickly Roots, "Fuck tha Police" by N.W.A., "Get the Fuck Out of Dodge" by Public Enemy, "Good Cop/Bad Cop" by Blahzay Blahzay, "Illegal Search" by LL Cool J, "In the Line of Duty" by Eightball and MJG, "One Time Gaffed 'Em Up" by Compton's Most Wanted, "Looking Through the Eye of a Pig" and "Pigs" by Cypress Hill, "Protect and Serve" by UGK, "Punk Police" by Mac Dre, "Say Hi to the Bad Guy" by Ice

Cube, "Sound of Da Police" by KRS-One, "Time for Us to Defend Ourselves" by MC Shan.

I want to get to my mom and I don't want to bring any attention to Ryan.

"Yes, officer." I bite my tongue. "I understand."

More cops show up, some in regular clothes. They make us sit on the side of the road, cuffed, while the K9 tears my car up.

Mr. Police, please try to see
That there's a million muthafuckas stressin just like me*

"Sorry, man. My bad." I feel like I let Ryan down, like I'm letting everyone down.

"It ain't your fault."

"If I would've just done the speed limit . . ."

"I can't run forever," he whispers.

"Well, I'll be damned," the officer says after they run everything. "You aware there is a warrant for your arrest?"

They take Ryan and vanish into the foggy night.

* "Only God Can Judge Me," 2Pac, 1996.

33

Brooklyn Girl

A bleak hospital is all hospitals. On the elevator up, I think about how I hate hospitals. The odor of the helpless, hopeless. The doctor is this pretty Indian lady. She tells me how my mom almost died.

I lean over Mom. She grabs my hand.

"I'm sorry, Ma," I keep saying. A million lights and indicators around her like NASA. I think about my brother, about me, and about her. About the last time she was healthy.

"Where were you?" she asks.

"A little bit of everywhere." She rubs my hand.

I stay with her, by her side, all day, all night. I dab her lips with the sponge-tipped water tube when her mouth gets dry. I want to make her happy.

I ask, "Were you ever happy? Like really happy?"

"Yes."

"When?"

She closes her eyes and grins.

"It was when my mother played Fats Domino records and closed her eyes when she danced . . . when every black girl wanted to look like Dorothy Dandridge and sing like Sarah Vaughan . . . when black girls were bronze, honey, tan, sepia, and black was the color of tar babies . . . when the Roxy was popping and all the brothers wore conks . . . Philly had the baddest jitterbugs and Detroit had the meanest gangs . . . when the blues was country and rock 'n' roll was city and they both was good for dancing . . . when my mother gave rent parties long after the rent was paid . . . when Easter meant new clothes and Cuban-heeled shoes and nobody seemed to mind that Jesus and the Easter bunny were white . . . when everybody went to church on Sunday no matter what happened Saturday night and Monday mornings belonged to the Man . . . when everybody knew they were colored and nobody wanted to be white—just don't call them black . . . when Mama rolled her hair up in paper curlers and everyone just knew she went to the beauty parlor . . . when nighttime was for lovers, and alleys and stoops were lovers' lane for a minute . . . when all old folks were grandma and grandpa and all children should stay out of grown folks' business . . . when I was everybody's child and had fifteen play aunts and uncles . . . It was when funeral homes gave out fans and drugstores gave out calendars and the corner store had a credit list just for Mama . . . when reading one book made you a bookworm and going to college made you damn near a genius . . . when certain things were said in front of white folks and white folks said everything . . . when we knew they weren't right but we didn't know nothing about our rights . . . when the weather was on our side and God only had one name . . . when prayers were answered and miracles were the order of the day . . . when children called grown folks "Miss Sarah" and "Brother James" and grown folks called children "sweetheart" and "honey" . . . when Mama used to wear circle skirts and scream when the wind blew her skirt up . . . when Daddy would slick his hair with Dixie Peach and then refuse to go out in the rain . . . when nobody touched the TV except for Daddy and nobody sat on the living room furniture except for company . . . when Grandma refused to wear her teeth and nobody complained . . . when everyone always had something to do and didn't mind doing it . . . when was it when everything was in place, or so it seemed? It was when little girls dreamt about growing up, and when was it that I grew up? When Mama talked about being respectable and Daddy talked about getting some . . . when home meant the projects, and when was it that the projects meant the ghetto? It was . . . a long time ago . . . when love was life and living was loving and everybody belonged to somebody."

I'm hugging on her, praying she can be happy again.

I think Uzi, my dad, and me are the reason she's in the hospital now. We did this to her, to us.

"What about school?"

Shrug. I tell her the truth.

"I dropped out."

She tells me about how important school is. How she had to fight for it. How it was for her, in Brooklyn, coming up.

"It's the only thing they can't take away from you," she says, "your education. Your passport for the future."

I tell her I would go back to school but Fels won't take me back.

"If I find a place—a school that will take you—will you go?" she asks.

I nod, anything for her.

34

The Alternative

It's called Crefeld.

"It's an alternative school," my mom says.

"Alternative?"

"Yes, alternative." She smiles. We're back in G-Town, together. I'm getting ready for my first day of school. When I leave, she's up, listening to music and sketching dances in her notebook.

My third school in three years.

Foes looked like shit.

Fels looked like jail.

Crefeld is perched on a hill and looks like a gingerbread house.

Kids shuffle in, the weirdest kids I've ever seen. A freak show: one white boy with a purple Mohawk and a neon green spiked dog collar; a group of kids draped in trench coats and dark ponytails, looking like Columbine shooters; little hippies barefoot in tie-dye; a Goth chick with her head shaved clean like G.I. Jane. A black kid with a blond Caesar and a huge Master lock around his neck. Most of these kids look like they're on strong meds. A handwritten sign reads: *Welcome to Crefeld, Home to the Mixed Nuts.*

I'm looking at these kids, thinking, *Alternative school? I'm not this damn alternative*.

"First day?" this kid asks.

"Yeah." I squint at him.

"I'm Dan." He looks Indian and has long tangly black hair with all types of ornaments—paper clips, charms, bottle caps, beads, keys—dangling off like a Christmas tree.

"Malo."

"Crefeld is like an island of misfit toys. Manufacturer rejects. Error cards."

"Yeah, well, not me. I'm normal."

"Normal, huh? Good luck with that." He treks up the hill.

Crefeld's the size of a mansion but inside feels busy like a row house. All the doors to the rooms are wide open. No bell, no guards, no metal detectors, everything here is different. They do this thing called Morning Meeting. People make announcements, eat muffins, sip tea. It feels like some camp I've never been to, like s'mores and sleeping bags.

"We need better snacks, Michael," Dan says. Other students join in, complaining about how there are no snacks and refreshments at the school.

Michael says, "Working on it." Michael's the principal! Everyone calls the teachers by their first name, it's wild. Debbie,

Dan, Stacey, Rena, Bill, Kevin, George, Greg. None of them look like teachers. They look more like surfers, skaters, hippies, and straight-up bums. The principal is rocking ripped jeans and sandals—Air Jesuses. There's a dog, Max, that lazes around.

This is written on the bench I'm sitting on:

Ten Tips for Being a Crefelder

10. Don't drink the water.
9. Shakespeare is kind of cool after a while, if you do drink the water.
8. Beware! If you ask Rena to sing, she will.
7. You'll dance to anything.
6. Lab reports are hard but you realize how wonderful learning is when you're not being force-fed.
5. Hyperactivity is contagious.
4. Introspections are harder.
3. You people are lunatics.
2. Never underestimate the value of eccentrics and lunatics.
1. Remember: With all its sham, drudgery, and broken dreams, it is still a beautiful world. Smile.

I smile for the first time in a long time.

35

The Blank Page

Stacey tells us to form a circle with our desks.

"A circle is a reflection of eternity," she says. Stacey's the English teacher. She's young with skin the color of art gallery walls and hair the color of tree bark. "Circles can't be broken. No beginning, no end, just motion."

There's only like a dozen kids in this class. This really short girl walks in late and sits next to me. If Amir was here—I miss him so much—he'd be like, *She so short she poses for trophies, so short she hang glides on Doritos, so short she does pull-ups on staples, so short she gives head standing up.*

Stacey sketches circles in the air. "If you put circles on top of each other, stack them up, you get a spiral." Stacey's big eyes search our faces to see if we follow. "Spirals are infinite."

"Pull out something to write on, something to write with: a pen, pencil, bloody fingernail." Everybody inks up. I don't have anything to write with. No paper either. I can't even remember the last time I did schoolwork.

Stacey puts a blank page down in front of me. Pen on top of it like a paperweight. "Okay, class, write!" Everyone in the class starts scribbling fast like reporters at a press conference. I just sit there, confused. She makes her way over.

"Write," she says, hawking over me.

"Write what?" I look around at everyone writing, lost in their own little worlds. I wonder what they're writing.

"Anything you want," she says.

"Anything I want?" I want to make sure I heard that right.

"Anything."

I know this trick. She's bullshitting. Teachers always tell you to express yourself, then when you really do, you get in trouble.

I write "Fuck school" and wait for her to flip. She's probably going to lose it, kick me out.

"Okay," she laughs. "Now keep writing. Keep going." *Ha, okay, since when?*

"Write your thoughts," she tells everyone.

"I'm trying," the short girl next to me, Ellen, says. "The only problem with writing my thoughts is that sometimes I don't know what I'm thinking."

I turn the page over. It's blank again.

The blank page is the starter pistol that fires and triggers my mind to sprint. *What will I write? What will I say? Will I say what I write, write what I say? Something funny? Some-*

thing serious? Something about my family? Something about Amir? Ryan? How will I start? Whose story will I tell? My story? Something made up? A story about a boy from Philly, a lost boy, who wants to find himself but doesn't know where to look, who wants to tell his story but doesn't know where to begin . . . or end, who searches anyway and discovers something about himself, the world?

Stacey reads from *The Pillow Book:* "'There are times when the world so exasperates me that I feel I cannot go on living in it for another moment and I want to disappear for good. But then, if I happen to obtain some nice white paper . . . I decide that I can put up with things as they are a little longer.'"

I stare at the blank page, an ocean of white alive with possibility.

I hear myself take a breath, then exhale—deep, like I just rose from underwater. It's like I'm at the free-throw line again. Foul shots. Like the game is on the line . . . again. I remember something my dad told me: *Shoot to make it*.

My hand shaking, trembling like it's freezing.

Then it hits: a silence louder than all the music I've ever heard in my life.

All the light in the world, in one beam, before me.

—

Pens dance to the beat of Stacey's voice: "Picture yourself writing . . . your mind moving . . . notice what you notice . . . catch yourself thinking . . . the purpose of writing is to stop time . . . what is the sound of one hand clapping? . . . writing synchronizes the mind, body, and spirit . . . open your mind and your mind's eye . . . only emotion endures . . . picture yourself writing . . ."

I grip the pen and something shoots down my spine, sits me straight up. The pen feels heavy, like it's made of stone.

At exactly which point do you start to realize
That life without knowledge is death in disguise?*

I stare deep into the blank page and see myself. I feel something I've never felt before: purpose. I don't know what my exact purpose is yet, but I know it has something to do with this pen and blank page. I am a blank page.

Holding the pen this way, snug and firm in my fist, makes me feel like I can write my future, spell out my destiny in sharp strokes.

But I can't write. So many things I want to write, but my pen is stuck, trapping my words like water under an ice block. The distance between my mind and the page feels like it could be measured in light-years.

* "K.O.S. (Determination)," Black Star, 1998.

—

"It's like there's a wall."

"Every wall is a door."

"You don't need to be great to get started, but you need to get started to be great." She sees my pen in the block of ice. "Try writing the first word that comes to your mind."

B-U-C-K.

buck (*n.*): a fashionable and typically hell-raising young man. 2 racial slur used to describe black men. 3 a young black man: *what's up young buck?* 4 the act of becoming wild and uncontrollable: *he went buck wild.* 5 a dollar. 6 to fire gunshots: *buck shots in the air.* 7 to go against, rebel: *buck the system*

36

Circle of Love

After free write, we share. She calls it the circle of love—you get a chance to read what you wrote. It kind of feels like what I imagine a campfire feels like, or an AA meeting.

We move around the circle.

SHAWN: "Orange-hued rainbow skies, eternal stormy summer nights, and stellar angel cloud dancing . . ."

SARAH: "If I were me, talking to me, I'd smack me already . . . It's funny how the intimidating are usually the intimidated . . ."

JOHN: "He's a politician. It's like being a hooker. You can't be a good one unless you can pretend to like people while you're fucking them."

RACHEL: "You raped my body but not my soul / Once broken, now I'm whole / You raped my body but not my mind / Can now see, was once blind . . ."

BECCA: "Feeling all alone / All alone at home / Going to school / Not acting very cool / Happy, sad, mad, no dad. Poem writing, lots of typing . . ."

AARON: "Rest my eyelids on the ride / Or get caught in riptide / If you like it french-fried / Be my bride. Seagulls dropping left and right, all night. All right. Okay, twine frays, repeated phrase, ruffled Lay's and sun rays in a haze . . ."

KATE: "There's hell in hello, good in goodbye, lie in believe, over in lover, end in friend, and ex in next so what's next . . . A true friend stabs you in the front . . . I have a shooting star on my wrist, means to go far. I have a heart on my hip it means to always love . . ."

TARA: "Amidst a hidden green hill / Tucked behind brass barriers far away / A figure is played on a windowsill / A daunting paragon of Irish beauty lay / Her pristine pale skin and soft pink cheeks / Frame large abyssal eyes / Which tell of the adventures she seeks / And imagines in the skies / Each cloud stretches and reaches / Satisfying her imagination / Natures she beseeches / To animate her creation."

GEOFF: "Money can't buy you love, but love can't buy you hookers . . . I would read my words but I'm being sued by Webster for plagiarism so . . ."

MALO: "I don't want to share."

"History admires the wise but elevates the brave," Dan says.

"And what does history say about assholes, yo?"

"I personally tend to have a lot of faith in assholes. My mom calls it self-confidence." I like Dan's sarcastic ass. He's witty and unafraid like Amir was.

—

I'm not ready to share, though. I just want to write.

After class I keep writing. School lets out and I'm still going, flowing, writing, writing. No one comes in. I hear Frank, the maintenance man, tell someone, "Yep, he's still in there, writing. Been in there for hours."

Next week it's the same thing: "Yep, he's still in there." I keep writing.

I write sentences that flow, like water, then I ride the word waves into new perceptions, new ideas.

I never thought I'd be voluntarily staying at school after school, but here I am. I realize that school and education don't go hand in hand, that school and education can be as distant or as close as sex and love.

The sun slopes across my face like a blessing. Falling rays light up the page and make my words glow.

37

Breakfast on J Street

I've been at Crefeld for a month now. Every day when I come home from school, my mom is out of her chair and off the meds. It's like watching a flower bloom. Today I come home to a dance studio. I walk in and am swept away—by sweet, sad symphonic strings, by mournful French horns, by a marching snare drum that ushers Amir into my thoughts, and by the silky sandpaper voice of Sam Cooke singing "A Change Is Gonna Come."

My mom directs two dancers, a guy and a girl, as they float around our little living room on tippy toes like black angels. The duo crash to the floor, then rise, jump in place, kick to the sky, and interlock like long-lost lovers, telling a story with their glistening bodies.

My mom cues their movements. "Ba-da-da ba-de-ba-da-ba-da . . . Ba-de-da-da-da," she sings. She's wearing a leotard and looks good. Her face glows like it's backlit. She stops the music and tells me they're preparing for some big dance competition. I can hear it in her voice—she wants it.

"Cross your fingers," the male dancer, Kemal, says.

"And . . . one of these is for you." My mom hands me two envelopes. I recognize Uzi's handwriting. I scream, "Yeah!" and jump around like I'm at a Cypress Hill concert.

The other letter is for Ted. I pocket my letter to read later and head out to give Ted his.

Back to 10 Gs.

I spot the crew, standing where they always stand, between the liquor store and the corner store, next to the Fern Rock Apartments fence, under the train tracks, and across the street from Rock Steady, this bugged ngh who sits on a crate all day with a broken radio, rocking his head back and forth to a beat no one else can hear.

Scoop and Ted both look gone. I give Ted the letter.

"Thanks, Malo. Where Uzi at? The crib?" Ted looks horrible. His Afro is dry and uneven, his clothes dirty, his speech slurred.

"He's locked up in Arizona," Scoop reminds him, wiping his drippy nose. "You know that." Scoop looks bad too, like he's aged ten years since I last saw him.

"Yeah, that's right . . . Yo, Malo, can you take us to get some breakfast?" Ted asks.

"Breakfast? You know what time it is?" I laugh.

"You know what I'm talking about." Actually, I don't.

"Where?"

“Down J Street,” Scoop says. “Come on, take us down there real quick.” I don’t feel like taking them, something tells me not to, but I do anyway.

Let freedom ring with a buckshot, but not just yet

First we need to truly understand the nature of the threat*

Jefferson Street looks like the “Thriller” video, all zombied out. Fiends, as thin as crack pipes, dance—the dancing dead—in the shadows and then, like Houdini, disappear . . . reappear somewhere else. Everything ghostly. Here—gone. Everybody’s eyes curry yellow or smog gray, dead as sunken ships.

This is where hope gone goes. It pulls hard at my spirit. I wonder what happened to Right Knowledge, to all that shit Ted was kicking last time.

The dealers chant inventory like a chorus:

“Crack out, crack out.”

“Coke out, coke out.”

“Her-ron, her-ron.”

“Ted Money,” one of the dealers yells, and rushes the whip. He pulls out a case with all different pills in it. “What you need?”

“Yo, right here?” I say, tapping Ted and checking my rearview for the jakes.

* “Nature of the Threat,” Ras Kass, 1996.

"It's cool, Malo, it's open air out here. Free market. No cops on J Street. Everything goes. Anything goes."

"Just got off, now imma 'bout to get on." I hear someone buzzing by. Shadows wipe past in stumbling zigzags.

"Bruce Lee," Ted shouts.

"Bruce Lee?" I look at Scoop.

"China White, heroin." *Ted's on heroin now? . . . The fuck?*

Black windows on boarded-up cribs like hollow eyes.

A fiend taps on my window. She looks like ET.

"I'll suck ya dick so good make ya ass lock up and snatch off da fitted sheet," she says . . . *The fuck?*

I roll the window back up.

In the rearview I catch Snoop snorting a line of coke off his fingernail.

"Want some of this eye-opener, Malo?" His head shoots back like whiplash.

"Pancakes," Ted says, holding the Xanax pills—zannies. "Syrup," with a Styrofoam cup full of lean—promethazine and codeine syrup. He drops the pills in the syrup. "Breakfast."

"Go ahead," Ted says, and passes the cup to me. "I call this shit the Incredible Hulk."

I look at it.

Look at them.

Pass.

—

I'm driving down Broad Street. Ted and Scoop are arguing, but the drugs got them on this crazy delay. Scoop will curse at Ted, but it takes Ted like thirty seconds to respond. It's like they're in outer space.

I'm mad at myself for even being here. It's fish-tank clear: nghz like Ted and Scoop can stay in my heart but not in my life.

Scoop's elbow brushes my face as he chokes Ted from the back. "Pussy!" Scoop shouts, and sits back in his seat hard. He lights a cig, zones out.

I yell, "Chill!" and focus on getting them back to Olney and the hell out of my whip.

After like a minute, Ted slurs: "You stabbed me, yo?"

I look and see the handle of a knife sticking out of Ted's chest.

". . . the fuck, Scoop?" I scream, swerving like I'm drunk.

Ted's whole shirt is dark and wet with blood, drenched like how Patrick Ewing's jersey is from sweat—

"Scoop?"

"Man, fuck that ngh!" he mumbles, taking a cold drag.

Ted just sits there, dazed and confused, bleeding, melting like a candle. I hit the gas, weaving in and out of traffic. I speed in the third lane, the gutter, racing to Albert Einstein Hospital.

"Hold on, man, hold on."

Woop-woop, woop-woop.

The police, hyena deep, surround the car.

Never again, I tell myself on my way to jail.

38

The Kite

"Another day in paradise," the guard says, looking at me like I'm a piece of shit.

They cuff Ted and take him to Einstein, book Scoop somewhere, and take me to a holding cell in the Thirty-fifth. This is the same place Uzi first got locked up at.

Think: *Every wall is a door.*

I'm biting my nails like they're sunflower seeds.

The cop that brought me in calls me "a piece of shit." It's cool. I ain't even mad at him. I mean, FTP all day, but it's really on me. On us, playing right into their hands like Play-Doh. Giving the cops and the prosecutors and the judges and the politicians who don't believe in us anyway exactly what they want.

Decisions lead to options, options to choices, choices to freedom. We all design our own reality, write our own script, build our own house . . . or prison . . . or coffin. Me Against

Law and Order is about being a true rebel, pushing against the grain, making my own path. Bucking the system.

I think about this show I saw on the Nature channel the other day about elephants. About how despite weighing up to twenty-five thousand pounds and standing thirteen feet tall, they can still be chained. *How?* I wondered. It starts when they're babies. Some asshole puts a metal chain attached to a wooden peg nailed into the ground around the baby elephant's foot. The baby elephant struggles but fails to break free and learns at that very moment not to struggle, that struggle is useless. Later on, even when the elephant can easily break free, it doesn't. I look around at all the sad hard gray black faces and see elephants.

Reaching for my wallet, RIP Amadou
I'm writing sentences like ya honor do
But I don't do the judging, no COINTEL,
I don't do the bugging, can't you nghz tell
Email to the system, Re: bel
I'm on some other shit like I'm on the mother ship*

They say I can go if a parent or guardian picks me up. I don't want to call my mom—she's feeling so good, this shit will bring her right back down. Haven't talked to my dad in forever, so I don't want to hit him up like this. I can't call him anyway because I don't even know his number.

I call Kianna, thinking about all the stories this phone must have. It just rings and rings, dry humming. I leave a message

* Me.

and wait in the cell. They drag people in all night. One guy, out of his mind drunk, with his forehead split open, is spinning around, spitting up, asking people to believe him.

"Please testify?" he says. "Will you testify for me?"

The only pull you got is the wool over your eyes
Getting knowledge in jail like a blessing in disguise*

I remember the letter my mom gave me before I went to 10 Gs, the one Uzi wrote to me. I find the envelope still there in my back pocket. I hear Uzi's voice:

Malo,

Wassup man? Hope everything is good with you, yo. I'm in this hellhole wondering my fate. When they transferred me here I wasn't 18 yet so I was on the 7th floor, where the other minors who have been transferred as adults are housed. We stayed in our cells 23 and 1, meaning we were in our cells for 23 hours a day and one hour out to take a shower and make a phone call. That shit makes u crazy, u find yourself thinking out loud, standing at your door for hours on end watching the guards watch you. I've read the whole Bible like 5 times cover to cover . . . Psalms is cool, keeps me calm. I'm still trying to get a Koran, but u know, this is Arizona! Haha. I can tell the fuckin time just by the way the sun hits my cell through my sun slit, which pretends to be a window . . . just by the shadows it casts on my cell walls. I'm on some monk shit.

I still can't get used to the constant noise in here man,

* "Respiration," Black Star, 1998.

it's something I can't explain, it's a fucking roar, a constant roar, like hard wind blowing in your ear all the time, u don't forget about it. People never stop talking, yelling, or screaming in here. I kind of think of it like how a black hole would sound, cuz this place is a void—a fucking hum of pain. The kids in there did some serious shit, mostly murder though. I used to think that a killer was a certain type of person. I now know that killing is an emotional reaction, cuz most killers aren't crazy people, shit is crazy.

The kid next door to me was an ese named Pelon, in for murder. He's in a gang outta Phoenix called Duppa Villa, his dad is in it, his mom is in it, this shit is like a right of passage to the eses, they take this shit in stride. When I first got here he gave me some food. Uncle Jabbar said in prison don't accept nothing from nobody, but fuck that, I was hungry! It was a Snickers bar and a bag of corn nuts, maaan that shit made me feel like I wasn't in jail anymore—just seeing the wrappers! Ain't that some shit? He sent it on a "kite." That's a long-ass string made from sock thread and boxer-short elastic . . . and that's how we send shit from cell to cell, letters, food, and other shit like that. When the guards see u doing it they take ya string from u, mothafukas go crazy when they get their strings took, it's like losing ya house phone!

On my 18th birthday, at midnight, three guards came to take me downstairs to the main jail general population. The muhfuka told me, "Happy birthday, kid, welcome to hell." The day before, Pelon passed off a shank to me made out of paper—yes, paper!—the shit is hard as metal and the shit has a spear point on it! Paper, yo! He told me they like to fuck with us young bucks cuz we're small and shit. He said if a punto fucks wit me bang em in the stomach right where the navel is. I feel that, but I just want to come home, Malo . . . but I guess I gotta do what I gotta do, yo.

Man, one thing I learned in here is that killas can be punks and punks can be killas, it don't matter. Just stand your square, never retreat—fuck that! If somebody wants to steal my respect, they gotta pay in blood, dog.

Pain is weakness leaving the body, Malo, remember that.

So yeah I'm in GP now with the adults, been here for a minute. They got me in the maximum-security block, red card status. It's better than the 7th floor shit, though. At least I can play ball, walk around, have some real human contact, and watch TV.

Out here on the West Coast they gangbang crazy, shit goes down every day. My cellie is my boy B-Brazy, he's a Blood from Mad Swan Blood Gang. We look out for each other, the ngh is down as shit. Check this: he never uses the letter *C*! When he talks he replaces the letter *C* with *B*, and when he writes he crosses out the letter *C* and anything else that reminds him of Crips! Hahahaha. There are like 10 Crips for every Blood, so Bloods be ridin hard with each other, cuz they r outnumbered. Because I roll wit Brazy, I'm what they call Bulletproof, 80 Proof, and Shotgun, meaning not Blood, but bangs with Blood . . . fuck it!

Uncle Jabbar said I'll probably do 5 years, I guess I can live with that. It's better than the 20 years the public defender told me I was facing when I was in juvie! I know one thing though, Malo, the boy in me has died, I've been forced to be a man. Mom and Dad can't help me in here, nobody gives a fuck about Afrocentricity or African dance in this jawn.

Malo, don't ever come to a place like this, it breeds violence, hate, and ignorance, and u never relax, u always have to watch what goes on around you, every little gesture, every word can b the difference between chilling or getting ya face tore off man . . . it's fucked up. It will change your "eyes"—do u get that? Ya spirit changes. The next time Mom sees me, she won't see her baby looking back at her, she will see someone else, someone different.

I've had a couple run-ins since I've been in here. I got into it with this OG Crip dude name Cisco Kaddafi. We were playing ball and the mothafuka kept hacking me. I got tired of it, and I threw my hands up at him. He told me, "Not here, we gonna do this at the pod." Brazy told me to "soap him," which means take bars of soap and put them in a sock as a weapon. When we got back to the pod, I b-lined for my hut, but he came to my door and said, "Naw, lil' loc, we gonna do this like g'z, ain't gonna be no weapons." I had to man up. We went to the showers and I just started swinging. Cisco is like 6′5″, 270, but I was connecting! . . . till he grabbed me though and slammed the shit outta me . . . but I got right the fuck back up . . . then the guards rushed in and choked us out on their SWAT team bullshit. They kept asking me if he attacked me, cuz he is known for shit like that. I was like "Fuck no! I attacked him!" even though it wasn't exactly like that. Haha. They wanted to know if I wanted to transfer to another cell block, or did I fear for my safety? What? Fuck no! I'm not a bitch, and I'm not gonna have a bitch jacket following me . . . in here u don't go out like that, even if it's not in ya best personal interest. They let me back in the pod and I was chillin. Cisco called me up to his cell, and was like "Yo, homie, I like ya heart," and he shook my hand. Then he gave two "tailor mades," which is a full cigarette, it's like giving someone 10 bucks.

See, Malo! Stand your square . . . Nghz respect u for that shit, no matter what! If u want my stripes, they not Velcro, u gotta rip my arm off to get them . . . yahmean!

I'm still writing my rhymes, though, I got this crazy-ass song called "24 Hours." The hook goes:

24 hours anotha soul loses power
Some bring sun rays, some dark days and showers
Some never see they visions so believe u blessed
Life is just a test u got the right to be stressed

But Malo, on some real shit, I wish I could go back to 707 and being a kid again, chillin in my room doing card tricks for you . . . hangin with Ted . . . u know? I wish me and u could rewind and play hanger ball in my room, or tracker wit Akil and Ahmed in the yard.

I've seen and heard too much, yo, it'll never be the same.

Think about the shit u do Malo, don't dick ride nobody, be yourself, and fuck drugs. Weed ain't a drug, though, it's spiritual stimuli . . . haha.

Protect Mom, pray for me, and sooner or later we will unite again.

Your bro, Uzi

39

Soul Food

Monday morning my dad comes to get me. He's standing at the desk, talking to one of the cops. He looks like he hasn't slept in a minute. I'm happy, mad, excited, nervous, anxious, thrilled, relieved, and angry to see him.

Outside the light hits me hard, squinting my eyes.

I can taste his disappointment. He can feel mine.

"What's your problem?" he asks me in the car, his angry Georgia eyes just staring straight ahead. The horizon is a trembling orange scarf. He doesn't even know that Amir is dead, that I'm not hanging with UPK anymore, that I'm writing, that I'm in school and I'm taking it seriously; all he knows is I got locked up. I do have a problem.

"You dumped your problems on me when you left."

"All separations are painful, it's the nature of things being ripped apart. When I left Valdosta at eleven to go to the Nashville Christian Institute it was painful. Tearing something away from something else is like that, but it doesn't have to be like that forever."

I can't help it. Everything he's saying is pissing me off. I'm angrier than I've ever been. I sit there and my blood just boils like my seat's a stove. I hear my mom's cries all those nights. I think about how we struggled. Fire in my eyes.

"I don't care what you have to say."

"You talking to me like that?" My dad squints in disbelief.

"Who else?" I'm starting to bite my lower lip. I taste my own salty blood. "Fuck you!"

"Trouble is a bitter tree, but sometimes it produces sweet fruits."

"What?"

"You're looking for trouble . . . and you found it," he says, pulling the car over.

"Talking to me like that you must want to squabble," he yells, his southern accent coming out.

"Let's go."

The car stops. We're at Broad and Erie in front of Checkers. He opens his door and is outside.

"Get on out here, then," he says, and slams the door. I come out and he's standing in front of me waiting for me to make a move. He's in a defensive stance like a wrestler. He probably hasn't rumbled since like the sixties. Amir would say, *He's so old he farts dust*. Amir would also say, *What are you doing? Man, at least you got a pop. At least he's trying. Nobody's perfect but at least he's in your life.*

For a second I can't believe we're doing this, but I throw my hands up anyway. I want to make him feel the pain me and my mom felt. I swing . . . he grabs me under my arms, I feel his strength as he lifts me off the ground while I beat his back with the side of my fist.

We're on the hood of the car. He's on top . . . now me . . . him . . . Cars roll by and honk peace. He's on top of me and looking straight into my eyes. It feels like he's looking right through to my soul. All my strength leaves. I can't move.

"I love you," he says hard under his breath, holding me down, pressing his words into me.

"Get off of me."

"I love you, boy," he yells now. I realize how much I missed his voice. We're panting, gasping for air.

We stay like that for a while, not fighting, just bonded, tangled together, and I feel at peace. Like we're one. Whole again.

"I'm so hungry" is how it ends. We walk across the street to Dwight's Soul Food.

BBQ chicken and catfish.

"Your mother and I were married in 1982 in Zimbabwe. She was the most incredible dancer I'd ever seen. Your birth was remarkable. I took her to the hospital twice in twenty-four hours and the second time you were born. You were the first American to be born in Zimbabwe. A true African American. You were celebrated and praised and held up as an example of African babyhood. Ministers of government and high officials like Makunike, Chimutengwende, and Shamuyarira blessed us and you. "

Mac and cheese and string beans.

"She suffered from hurts from childhood that I knew little about and could not repair regardless of my actions, love, and devotion. She had been brutalized by others, from what she told me, but I never treated her brutally nor ever raised my hand toward her. I loved her. I thought I could help her control it. I was the first person to insist that she go see a psychiatrist, which she did. I was with her when the top psychiatrist in the country declared that she was manic-depressive and prescribed lithium right on the spot. She had a couple of major surgeries that caused her to go into a deeper depression."

Yams and corn bread.

"She started spending money we didn't have, paying far too much money for things that we either did not use or did not need. She didn't want me to know that she had been stretching money from one place to pay another, using more than twenty credit cards to handle the juggling. Neither your mother nor I could survive in misery. We struggled to pay your tuition. Each month we got deeper into debt."

Black-eyed peas and collard greens.

"The day I left I believed that I was making the best decision I could. My commitment to you has never wavered. I have always thought that my responsibility was first to my children. I have never wished your mother any harm or ill. None of us choose our own demons."

Hush puppies and okra.

I'm listening to his story but it doesn't matter anymore. I don't care what he's saying, only about him . . . and my mom . . . and Uzi and where we all go from here. Amir was right—I'm lucky to have a dad who cares, who's down to fight with me, for me, for us.

"I love you," I say for the first time in years. He tells me his love for me is unconditional.

Sweet potato pie.

On the way home, he plays a speech from his friend Jeremiah in Chicago: "What makes you so strong, black man? How is it that three hundred and seventy years of slavery, segregation, racism, Jim Crow laws, and second-class citizenship cannot wipe out the memory of Imhotep, Aesop, Akhenaton, and Thutmose II? What makes you so strong, black man? . . . How is it that after all this country has done to you, you can still produce a Paul Robeson, a Thurgood Marshall, a Malcolm X, a Martin King, and a Ron McNair? What makes you so strong, black man? . . . This country has tried castration and lynching, miseducation and brainwashing. They have taught you to hate yourself and to look at yourself through the awfully tainted eyeglasses of white Eurocentric lies, and yet you keep breaking out of the prisons they put you in. You break out in a W. E. B. Du Bois and a Booker T. Washington. You break out in a Louis Farrakhan and a Mickey Leland; you break out in a Judge Thurgood Marshall and a Pops Staples; you break out in a Luther Vandross, Magic Johnson, Michael Jordan, Harold Washington, or Doug Wilder. What makes you so strong, black man?"

40

The Most Beautiful Country

The blank page begs me to tell a story—dares me to tell one—one that's never been told before, and to tell it like it will never be told again.

The blank page lights up a room in my heart that I didn't know existed.

I'm standing outside of Crefeld, staring into the endless green of Wissahickon Park, when my purpose finds me.

I hear Uncle Howard's voice in my head as I race through the hallway: *Let the beauty of what you love be what you do.*

This is the come up, writing to the sun come up
I never get enough of the nighttime, so I write lines
That rhyme over linoleum beats, for kids scrolling them streets
Conquer the beast, cock and release*

* Me.

I find Stacey in her classroom.

I declare it: "I want to be a writer."

"That's great, Malo," she says, moving to the bookshelf. A sign above the bookshelf reads: *Every blade of grass has its angel that bends over it and whispers, "Grow, grow."*

She pulls out a book and says, "Means you have to be a good reader, though." She hands me *On the Road* by Jack Kerouac.

That night, sitting on the terrace overlooking G-Town, I enter the world of Sal Paradise and Dean Moriarty as they wander across the highways of America, just like me and Ryan did a few months back, finding adventure and trouble and girls and drugs and themselves all at once.

The next day I ask Stacey for another book.

She chuckles. "How about finishing *On the Road* first?"

"I did." She looks at me like she wants to believe me but doesn't. She squints for me to 'fess up. I pull the words from the back of my eyes: "'The only people for me are the mad ones, the ones who are mad to live, mad to talk, mad to be saved, desirous of everything at the same time, the ones who never yawn or say a commonplace thing, but burn, burn, burn like fabulous yellow roman candles exploding like spiders across the stars.'"

I tell her I didn't just read *On the Road,* but that I understood it, related to Sal and Dean's journey, what they were feeling, their quest for freedom and dream chasing.

—

She gives me a stack of books.

I devour them, finishing a book a day. I push myself hard because I feel like I'm behind, like I have to make up for lost time. Before Crefeld, the last book I read was in sixth grade. I starved myself and now I'm hungry for words, phrases, stories, and knowledge. The more I read, the more I want to read.

José Martí, a Cuban writer from back in the day, says literature is the "most beautiful country." For me, each book is a journey, a voyage into new land.

I finish Stacey's stack and hit the library. A sign above the entrance says *Lys Ce Que Voudra (Read What You Will)*. And that's what I do. I walk through the aisles of books, touching spines with my fingertips, rubbing dust jackets with my thumbs, and reading everything with my heart.

WHITMAN: "Take off your hat to nothing known or unknown or to any man or number of men, go freely with powerful uneducated persons and with the young and with the mothers of families, read these leaves in the open air every season of every year of your life, re-examine all you have been told at school or church or in any book, dismiss whatever insults your own soul, and your very flesh shall be a great poem and have the richest fluency not only in its words but in the silent lines of its lips and face and between the lashes of your eyes and in every motion and joint of your body."

—

GINSBERG: "I saw the best minds of my generation destroyed by madness, starving hysterical naked, dragging themselves through the negro streets at dawn looking for an angry fix, angelheaded hipsters burning for the ancient heavenly connection to the starry dynamo in the machinery of night, who poverty and tatters and hollow-eyed and high sat up smoking in the supernatural darkness of cold-water flats floating across the tops of cities contemplating jazz."

I spend a night at my dad's apartment in Levittown. It's small, even smaller than my mom's spot in G-Town, and barely furnished. I crash on the futon in the living room. He cooks eggs, grits, and toast in the morning. I eat slow, savoring each bite like it's my last. Over breakfast I tell him that I want to be a writer. He tells me that writing is in my DNA, that my grandfather loved to write.

"He was always a man to speak his mind," he remembers, leaning back in his chair. "I remember when I realized I had to return to Georgia to see him. It was when he told me on the phone, 'I can't hold the pen anymore.' That was the most frightening thing I had ever heard him utter because he wrote something every day, a tradition that he started after finding himself confined to his bedroom. It was in his blood to speak his mind and to have his say. If he could not speak it vocally to an audience, he would write sermons and poems and songs. And he did so until the day he could not hold the pen, the day he died."

Before I bounce to go back to Philly, Pops gives me a few books: *Assata, The Autobiography of Malcolm X, The Miseducation of the Negro*. The books show the world not just as it is but as it could be, should be. They connect me to everything that has ever happened and to everyone who has ever lived.

WOODSON: "When you control a man's thinking you do not have to worry about his actions. You do not have to tell him not to stand here or go yonder. He will find his 'proper place' and will stay in it. You do not need to send him to the back door. He will go without being told. In fact, if there is no back door, he will cut one for his special benefit. His education makes it necessary."

BALDWIN: "People pay for what they do, and still more for what they have allowed themselves to become. And they pay for it very simply; by the lives they lead."

DU BOIS: "Now is the accepted time, not tomorrow, not some more convenient season. It is today that our best work can be done and not some future day or future year. It is today that we fit ourselves for the greater usefulness of tomorrow. Today is the seed time, now are the hours of work, and tomorrow comes the harvest and the playtime."

FANON: "Who am I? Am I who I say I am? Am I all I ought to be? . . . Each generation must, out of relative obscurity, discover its mission, fulfill it, or betray it."

—

HURSTON: "The present is an egg laid by the past with the future inside its shell."

WHITMAN: "Do I contradict myself? Very well, then I contradict myself, I am large, I contain multitudes."

DEVLIN: "We were born into an unjust system; we are not prepared to grow old in it."

BALDWIN: "We live in an age in which silence is not only criminal but suicidal . . . for if they take you in the morning, they will be coming for us that night."

BAKER: "Give light and the people will find their own way."

Now I see why reading was illegal for black people during slavery. I discover that I think in words. The more words I know, the more things I can think about. My vocab and thoughts grow together like the stem and petals of a flower. Reading was illegal because if you limit someone's vocab, you limit their thoughts. They can't even think of freedom because they don't have the language to. I think about all the nghz I know with limited vocabs, the ones who keep asking, *Nahmean? Yahmean?* because they don't have the words to express what they really mean. I don't want to fall into that trap, so every day I learn new words: *ascetic, mizzenmast, aft, estuary, diaphanous, sedentary, trireme, drapetomania.*

ASSATA: "People get used to anything. The less you think about your oppression, the more your tolerance for it grows. After a while, people just think oppression is the normal state of things. But to become free, you have to be acutely aware of being a slave."

Against all odds, the math's off
Forcing us into the night
Where we bargain with death for discounts on life
We get half-off*

I read *Animal Farm* and think about all the crooked cops in Philly.

ORWELL: "The creatures outside looked from pig to man, and from man to pig, and from pig to man again; but already it was impossible to say which was which."

I read Sistah Souljah and think about Nia: "Only a hard-working man, a sharp thinker who doesn't hesitate to do what he gotta do, to get you what you need to have, deserves you."

* Me.

—

SIDDHARTHA: "Make the effort to obtain information that will allow you to best guide your destiny. Make your voice heard in the world through your life and works and do not be lowered into inaction by status, tradition, race, ethnicity, gender, or affiliation. Do not believe in anything simply because you have heard it. Do not believe in anything simply because it is spoken and rumored by many. Do not believe in anything merely on the authority of your teachers and elders. Do not believe in traditions because they have been handed down to many generations. But after observation and analysis, when you find that anything agrees with reason and is conducive to the good and benefit of one and all, then accept it and live up to it."

I write in between reading. I write everything: poems, rhymes, stories, essays. Sometimes what I want to say is a poem, sometimes it's a story, a movie, or a song. Each form of writing is like its own language. I want to be fluent in all of them so that I can speak to people in whatever language they understand.

Stacey says being a good writer is about making connections, connecting the dots. I start connecting everything back to writing. Like how in science class today, George, my science teacher and basketball coach, was talking about the difference between a thermostat and a thermometer. The thermostat changes the temperature; the thermometer just reflects it. I want my writing to be like a thermostat.

Writing is just like the streets: don't hide anything at the beginning, don't reveal anything until the last possible moment.

41

Y2K Hustle

Y2K hangs on the horizon like sunset. The supermarket shelves are empty. Gas station lines look like rush hour traffic. Everybody's stocking up on everything, panicking, bracing for the last days. It's like that Prince song: *And tonight we're gonna party like it's 1999*. Action News 6 says all the world's computers are going to crash. I think about 10 Gs and how their spaceship, Nibiru, is supposed to come and take them away on Y2K.

Despite all the Y2K chaos, word on the street is that Bone and Damien are still gunning for me. "Dead man walking," they call me.

Kam tells me this on the phone. His voice cracks with fear. "So what you gonna do?"

I don't know. Philly's only so big and I'm bound to run into them eventually. My brain storms on legal ways to get money . . . not just to pay Bone off, but for myself and to help my mom.

I head back to Olney.

A hustler, an entrepreneur, is about seeing opportunities and seizing them. Like 2Pac said, a real N.I.G.G.A. is Never Ignorant Getting Goals Attained. It's about looking around and peeping all the possibilities. The entrepreneur sees the world as the writer sees the blank page—as a chance. The game changes but the hustle stays the same.

I walk into Fresh Cutz and find Mike. He tells me that there's a few people in front of me, waiting for haircuts.

"I'm not here for a cut," I say.

"What's up?"

I reach into my pockets and grip all the money I have in the world.

"You still got those vending machines?"

42

Full Circle

I watch my classmates stock up on snacks before class. Juice, soda, water, candy, chips, cookies, crackers, gum, all courtesy of my vending machines. I pitched the vending machine idea to my school—"It's what the students want," I told Michael, "supply and demand"—and they green-lighted it. I stock up on product at Sam's Club for a nice discount, fill my machines up, and voilà!

Wrappers crinkle around the circle of love. The whole class chomping and munching and slurping. In the circle of love, I come out first: "I want to read."

All eyes on me.

"This is a story I've been working on . . . I'm not done yet . . ."

This is it.

—

"The fall in Killadelphia. Outside is the color of corn bread and blood. Change hangs in the air like the sneaks on the live wires behind my crib. Me and my big brother, Uzi, in the kitchen . . ."

I get home from school, my mom rushes me, pushing a letter into my hand.

"Read it," she says, antsy.

I unfold it, thinking it's probably from Uzi.

I read under my breath: " 'Dear Amina . . . demonstrated exceptional capacity for exceptional creative ability in the arts . . .' " I stop reading and smile at her. "You won?"

"I won! I got it."

My hug tells her how proud I am of her. I think about how strong she is to win something like this in the midst of all the chaos and sickness. She's like Jordan in the flu game.

Glowing in the dark like a fuzzy star in the black night, the TV says, "The big story on Action News tonight . . . It's being called one of the biggest drug and weapons busts in Philadelphia history . . . three suspected drug and weapons dealers have been arrested in a million-dollar criminal operation . . ." They show Bone and Damien being hauled into police headquarters in cuffs. Bone has his T-shirt pulled up over his face.

They flash his mug shot. It's surreal. I think about how that could have been me. The TV shows the police behind a table with all of the drugs, money, guns, and ammunition they seized. I think about how Bone and Damien wanted to kill me, tried to kill me, and maybe they even killed Amir? I think about how Nia warned me all of this would happen, how she loved me enough to say something.

I remember what she told me: *Love is learning the song in someone's heart and singing it to them when they forget.*

43

The Five Spot

Black Jesus mosaic looking right at me. I'm sitting in the pews of Bright Hope Baptist Church waiting for Nia, watching her choir rehearsal.

"That's the largest stained-glass black Jesus in the world," one of the church elders whispers to me under "Go Tell It on the Mountain." *Go, tell it on the mountain / Over the hills and everywhere* . . . Sun pours through.

Nia sees me when I come in, sees me, and it's like when we first locked eyes at Broad and Olney.

I'm not the average savage that curse queens
I'm something from his worst dreams*

We watch Y2K fireworks explode, big and bright like electric sunflowers in the night sky, above the Art Museum.

* "Don't See Us," The Roots, 1999.

Our hands interlocked, I apologize to her.

"Everybody is going to hurt you in some way," she says. "You just got to find the ones worth suffering for. And I did."

"Thank you." She says that *espera,* the Spanish word for "waiting," comes from the word *esperanza*—"hope." She asks if I see the connection.

"I feel it."

She tells me about this concept the Mayans have: *in lak esh,* meaning "You are my other me and I am your other you."

"In lak esh," she says.

I look into her eyes and see all the seasons changing at the same time.

"Malo, do you know what my name means?" Nia asks.

"No."

"Purpose."

Time passed, we back in Philly now she up in my spot
Tellin me the things I'm tellin her is makin her hot*

Nia leads me through the darkness of Old City. We walk past a smelly place called Bank Street Hostel, cut across a parking lot, and end up standing in an alley under a colorful flag that says *The Five Spot*. It feels like a secret place. Outside the entrance is alive with energy. Cyphers, laughter, the click of heels on concrete, and music from inside pours out like warm air.

* "You Got Me," The Roots, 1999.

"If you can walk, you can dance. If you can talk, you can sing," the host says. "Poetry is the voice of a sea animal living on land, wanting to fly in the air."

One mic, glowing onstage like the most precious jewel in the diamond district. It's dim, crowded. A spotlight throws a beam around like a lighthouse.

All types of peeps in here: races, styles, vibes. Beautiful brown girls with Coke hips and tribal tats. Backpackers with backward fitteds and notebooks. Divas in dresses, long legs, pointy shoes. Braids, dreads, weaves, perms, baldies, everybody nappy, happy.

The host spots Black Thought, ?uestlove, and the band. "The legendary Roots crew from Philadelphia!"

It's an open mic. Anybody can go up and rip it. A blur of underground talent blesses the stage. Poets Black Ice, Ursula Rucker, Post Midnight, Just Greg rip it. Emcees Bohemian Fifth, Suga Tongue Slim, and King Syze rock the mic. Then this lady, Jill Scott—"Jilly from Philly" they call her—sings, brings the damn house down, and gets a standing O.

Nia sings "Tell Him" by her favorite singer, Lauryn Hill. Her lips glow as she sings. People ad-lib: *Get it girl, get it . . . tell him . . . uh-huh, don't stop . . . work, girl.*

"Now if you don't like that," the MC says, "then something is wrong with your eardrum, your anvil, and your damn hammer!"

"Next up to the stage . . . Malo," the MC calls out. Nia must have written down my name. She smiles and claps for me to go up.

—

BALDWIN: "Your crown has been bought and paid for, all you must do is put it on your head."

I walk up to the stage. It reminds me of the blank page. I start with the word I wrote in Stacey's class: *Buck*.

Young buck, buck wild,
buck shots, buck town
Black buck, make buck
slave buck, buck now

Buck fitty, buck block,
buck down, buck sacred
go buck, buck me,
buck system, buck naked

The drummer from the house band starts drumming a beat for me. I flash a smile at Nia. Over the deep call of the drum, I respond with my story:

G-Town, '98, me and my mother
and mother-fuck the cops, they knocked my brother
He's state-roadin it, 23 and 1
Telling time by the shadows of the sun

Sis in psych ward, seeing neighbors
And I stay suspended, fuckin behavior
No savior, just danger
And Pops left so now I got the banger

Man of the house, North Philly to South
And my ol' heads punched me in my young mouth
They told me to get up—I got up
They told me to hustle—I got my knot up

Outside, pulling my socks up and
Bombing on anybody that's not us
In Illadel, where they shoot the cops up
Shoot, it's that, or get locked up

Dreams like ground balls, they don't pop up
Getting rocked up to get locked down
And where them daddy's at?
They don't come around

And where that message at?
(W)rapped underground
Searched the streets for myself
Lost and found

The audience starts clapping, snapping, and nodding to the beat. The whole Five Spot trembles with rhythm.

Uzi in the cage filled with rage
Best friend murdered—all I got is this page
And Pops' 12-gauge, few options
They on J Street, tossin toxins

Purple rain cuz the pain knockin
But I can't afford to bug my mind frame

If you saw how far my mind came
And could see how far my mom came

Then you could understand my grind frame
Hustle insane in the Langston Hughes lane

Known rivers, ancient dusky
Known devils too, tryna corrupt me
Get me to sell my soul for a couple dollars
Not knowin I got the mind of a couple scholars

And a few hustlas, child of Black Power,
The move meant to move this, I'm fluent
Shapes and shadows—my angles congruent
Missing student, most times I was tru-ant

Peep the distance
'Tween education and schoolin
See the difference
One frees, one ruins

Most of the audience is on their feet now, throwing adlibs and affirmations onstage, encouraging me.

Auto focus with a Canon lens
Love the hood but I feel like I'm gamblin
Might get lucky, no Peterson
And fuck blind haters who can't see me win

Love of my life: secret ingredient
Good bruva but always so deviant

Late at night, ridin on the median
And fuck the news—time to ride on the media

I follow nobody just leadin ya
Toothbrush rap, tracks reachin ya
On all cylinders, you numb, you ain't feelin this
Inauthentic if you can't see the real in this

Not hit or miss it's—just hit or hit
Me and cousins in the Bronx in the pits
Tracy Tow brown foul, been a while now
And all the wild childs Rikers Isle pen pals

Come again now? How we get to this?
Generation where we proud of our ignorance?
And common sense ain't common—just call it sense
Life or death, stop ridin the fence

Killadelphia, Pistolvania
Where they clap at strangers
And spit poetry like a banger
I learned how to play ball on a hanger

They used to cut ya balls off when they hang ya
Balls like these so rare they endangered

So I'm ready, armed and deadly
My mind is my sword—I'm edgy

I polish these odes to conquer my Foes
Break the beat down, demolish the flow

On the road, driving fast
Young King, free at last . . . So
Miss me with the bullshit, like how them
Shells missed me when that tool spit

Lunar eclipse, I'm moonlit
Wasn't headed nowhere, now I'm movin
Wasn't doing nothin, now I'm doin

Became a doer, dream pursuer, purpose-driven
Past meets the future
In between no longer and not yet
Rise up, young buck, never forget

44

Bearing Fruit

Graduation. Birds crisscrossing above our heads. The audience is under a white tent. The graduates, we're out baking in the loud June sun.

The graduation is laid-back, like everything else at Crefeld. It feels like a picnic or a family reunion. My mom, overflowing with joy, is the star of the show. Her smile, an endless flood of white light, is set in stone.

Present is a gift, that's why it's called present
Troubled adolescence had my mom stressin
Now a different story, Doris Lessing
No matter where I go from here, Philly reppin*

* Me.

My dad sits next to her. It's the first time they've been together, in the same place, since he left. I smile at both of them and inhale summer.

All of my teachers are here: George, Kevin, Debbie, Stacey.

George speaks to our class: "Ralph Ellison once said, 'I don't know what intelligence is. But this I do know, both from life and from literature: whenever you reduce human life to two plus two equals four, the human element within the human animal says, "I don't give a damn." *You* can work on that basis, but the kids cannot. If you can show me how I can cling to that which is real to me, while teaching me a way into the larger society, then I will not only drop my defenses and my hostility, but I will sing your praises and help you to make the desert bear fruit.' "

45

Rivers

A scarf wrapped around my head like the locals. No clouds, just 120 degrees of Egyptian sun. It glows above the desert like a giant halo. My Timbs are the color of the pyramids I'm standing in front of.

"Welcome home, my Nubian brother," the sellers yell, pushing product in my face. It's all smiles, love, can't knock the hustle.

"You were born on this continent," my dad says.

Me and my pops: riding camels with colorful Persian rug humps, kicking up sand in front of the Sphinx at Giza; steering little boats down the Nile while old men with ancient feet and smiles wider than the river watch and laugh from the grassy banks; crawling into limestone to see etchings older than everyone I've ever met combined; mazing through huge columns that shoot up into the sky like space shuttles; seeing the dusky black faces on the walls of the history they don't teach in school; and eating *ta`meyya* and laughing into the night.

I pull Amir's chain out of my pocket. I see his smoky face in the silver.

SHONAGON: "When you have gone away and face the sun that shines so crimson in the East, be mindful of the friends you left behind, who in this city gaze upon endless rain."

We end up in Abu Simbel. It's early morning. The call for prayer goes out and sounds like an ancient song. I think all prayer should sound like a song.

> **Inject the thesis, spoke to my pops and left him speechless**
> **He saw me sprout, goin through worlds that wore me out***

We walk down a hill, along a mountain, and then turn to face it.

Facing the mountain. Four faces, huge black faces with crowns, cast into an enormous limestone cliff.

A tour guide tells a group in front of us, "These colossal statues were sculpted directly from the mountain, cut from the natural rock of the mountain . . ."

I think about that: how these bold, brilliant faces were

* "How Ya Livin," AZ featuring Nas, 1998.

trapped inside the mountain the whole time . . . waiting to be discovered, waiting to reveal the beauty underneath, waiting to be seen, waiting like an untold story. I see my family in the stone faces.

"The young, handsome face is finely carved. He wears a crown on his head . . . The line of the smiling lips is more than a meter long," the guide goes on.

I am the mountain and the sculptor, losing myself, finding myself, revealing what was there all along.

HUGHES: "My soul has grown deep like the rivers."

We stand there, together, at the peak of one mountain and the foot of another, facing the rising sun.

Much Love

To the Most High and the ancestors.

To my mother and father for their unshakable love.

To my big brother for showing me how to rise and shine.

To Maya, my queen, and Aion, my prince, for their divine light.

To Ben Haaz, Jan Miller, and Lee Steffen for helping make this book a reality.

To my editor, Chris Jackson, for being brilliant. To my publishers Cindy Spiegel and Julie Grau, and Random House for providing a platform for me to tell my story.

To my sister, Eka. To my cousins: Ahmed, Akil, Nikia, and Chris. My aunts: Sylvia and Georgia. My uncles: Howard, Abdul, and John. My nephew Nasir. To the Freelon family.

To my teachers and mentors: Joel Wilson, Kevin Howie, Deb Sotack, Debbie Nangle, Stacey and Dan Cunitz, George Zeleznik, Charles Fuller, Owen Alik Shahadah, Lawrence Ross, Saul Williams, Jim Brown, Kenny Gamble, Walter Lomax, Kofi Opoku, Samuel Hay, Ian Smith, Lee Upton, Maya Angelou.

To my team: Nina-Marie Nunes, Jeff Schuette, David Sloan, Dwight Watkins, Rassaan Hammond, Errol Webber, Ryan Bowens, and Jeffery Whitney.

To my homies: Jon, Dustin, Jordan, King Syze, Shalana, Ted, Scoop, D-Rock, Struggle, and King Mez.

To my extended family all around the world for their support and encouragement.

To my brothers and sisters locked down (they can't imprison your soul!).

To the voiceless whose voice I evoke through pen strokes.

To Philly, my city. To hip-hop, my sound track.

To you.

ABOUT THE AUTHOR

MK Asante is an award-winning writer, filmmaker, professor, and hip-hop artist. A recipient of awards from the Academy of American Poets and the Langston Hughes Society, he is the author of the seminal hip-hop text *It's Bigger than Hip Hop* and the poetry collections *Beautiful. And Ugly Too* and *Like Water Running Off My Back*. He directed *The Black Candle,* a Starz TV movie he co-wrote with Maya Angelou, who also narrates the prize-winning film. He wrote and produced the film *500 Years Later,* winner of five international film festival awards as well as UNESCO's Breaking the Chains award.

Asante studied at the University of London, earned a BA from Lafayette College, and an MFA from the UCLA School of Film and Television. Asante has lectured and performed in over thirty countries as well as throughout the United States at hundreds of colleges, universities, libraries, concerts, and festivals. He was awarded the Key to the City of Dallas, Texas. His essays have been published in *USA Today,* the *Huffington Post, San Francisco Chronicle*, and the *New York Times*.

Asante is a tenured professor of creative writing and film in the Department of English and Language Arts at Morgan State University.

mkasante.com

ABOUT THE TYPE

This book was set in Sabon, a typeface designed by the well-known German typographer Jan Tschichold (1902–74). Sabon's design is based upon the original letter forms of Claude Garamond and was created specifically to be used for three sources: foundry type for hand composition, Linotype, and Monotype. Tschichold named his typeface for the famous Frankfurt typefounder Jacques Sabon, who died in 1580.